Monterey, California, is situated on the southern shores of the famed Monterey Bay, a five-mile deep twenty-mile wide half moon south of Half Moon Bay and San Francisco. To its south, lies the famed town of Carmel with galleries galore and restaurants to die for. From then on, if on a drive, you can survive the most beautiful stretch of land in the world called Big Sur (Big South) to Hearst Castle, named after the newspaper tycoon and spot on center of the casting for the great Citizen Kane, a film made by Orson Welles. Are there ghosts in Monterey? You tell me. And please tell John Steinbeck as well.

# *The Ghosts Of Monterey*

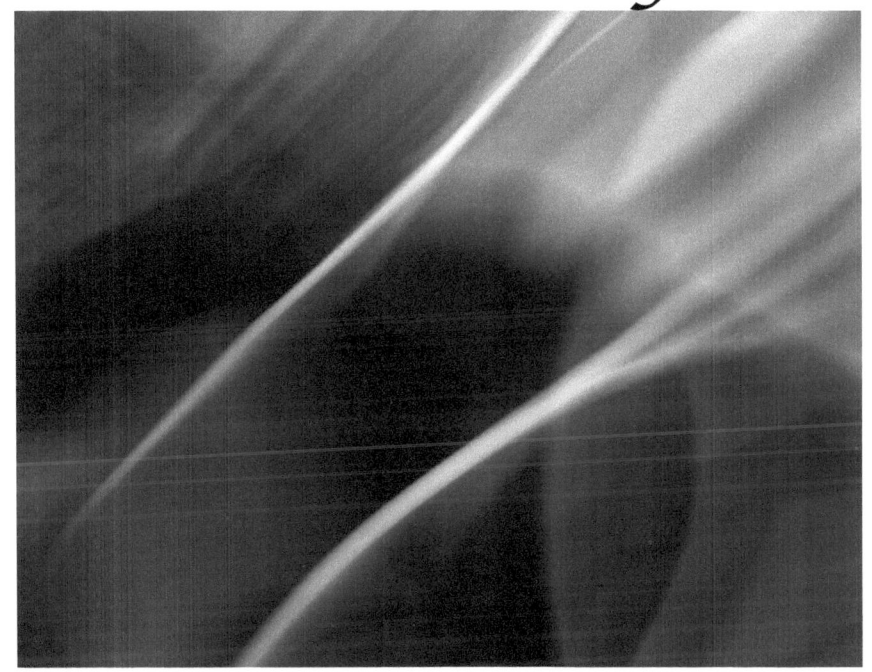

# Photographs
# By
# David Cope

The Ghosts of Monterey
Photographs by David Cope

Epoc Books
Printed in the United States of America
© David Cope 2016
All Rights Reserved.
Published 2012.

This book is dedicated to my wife, sons, and grandchildren,
Zoe, Tess, Gavin, and Ethan whose excitement for everyday
things never ceases to amaze me. And to those older kids like
me who believe in those children.

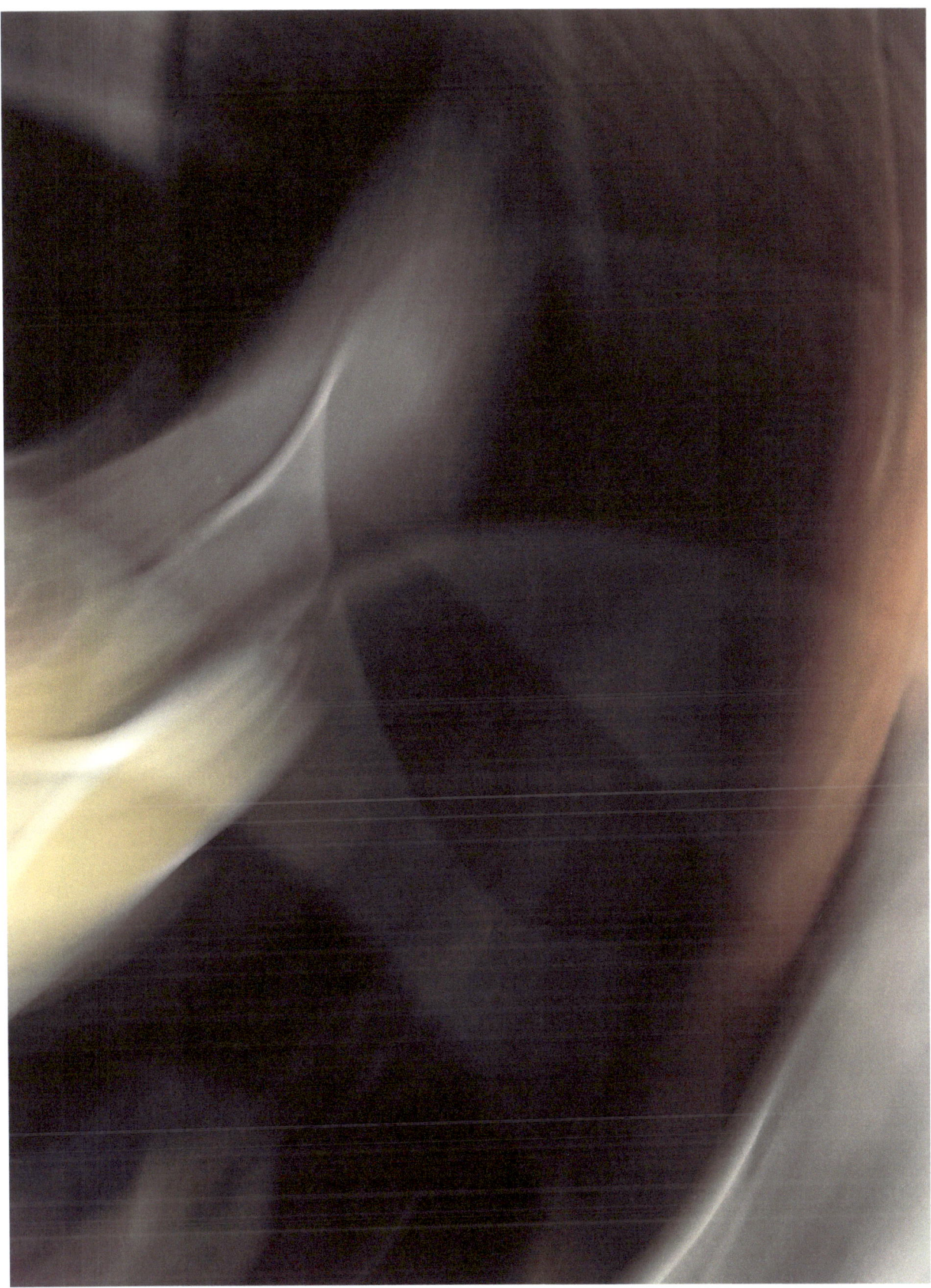

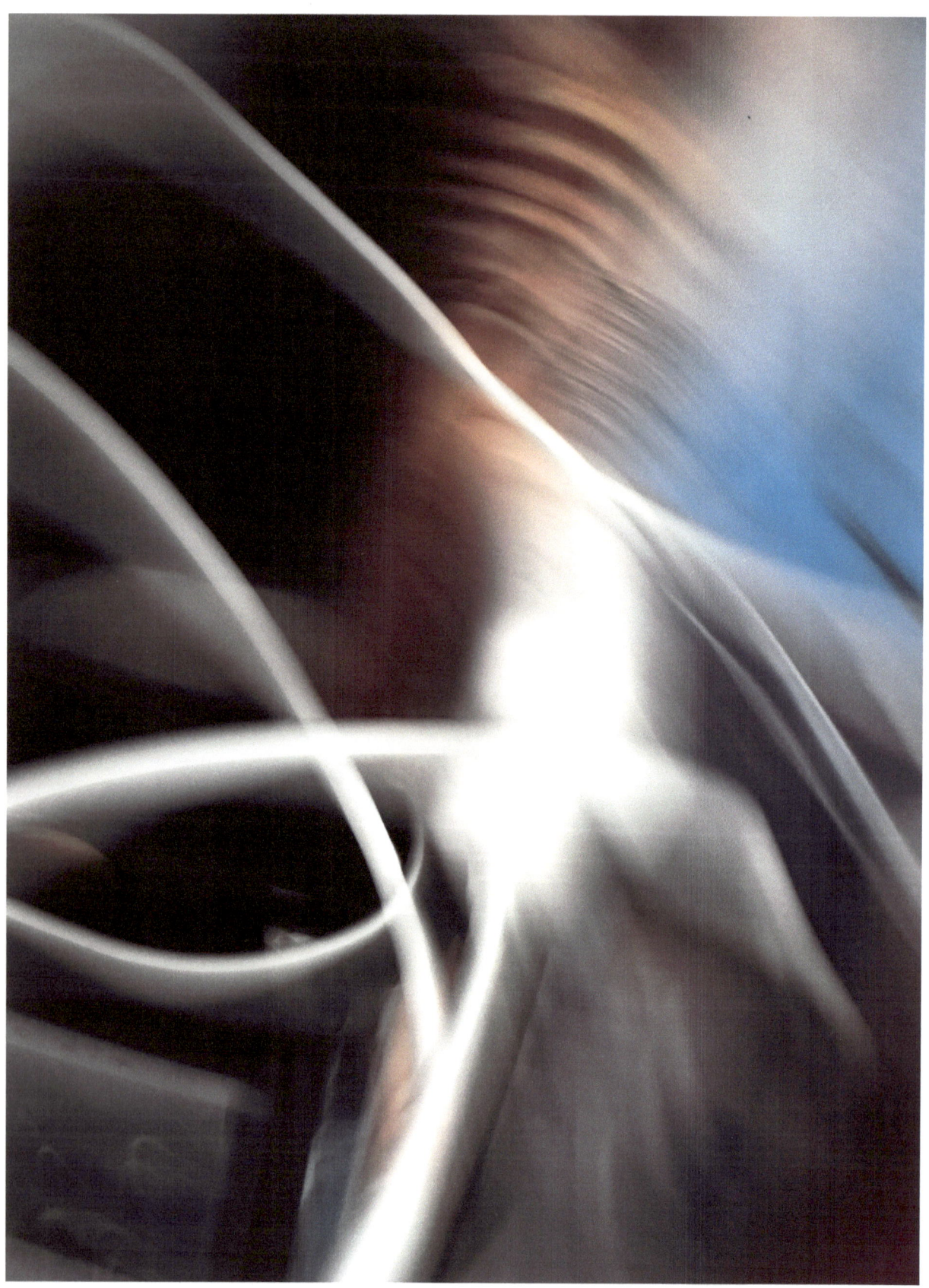

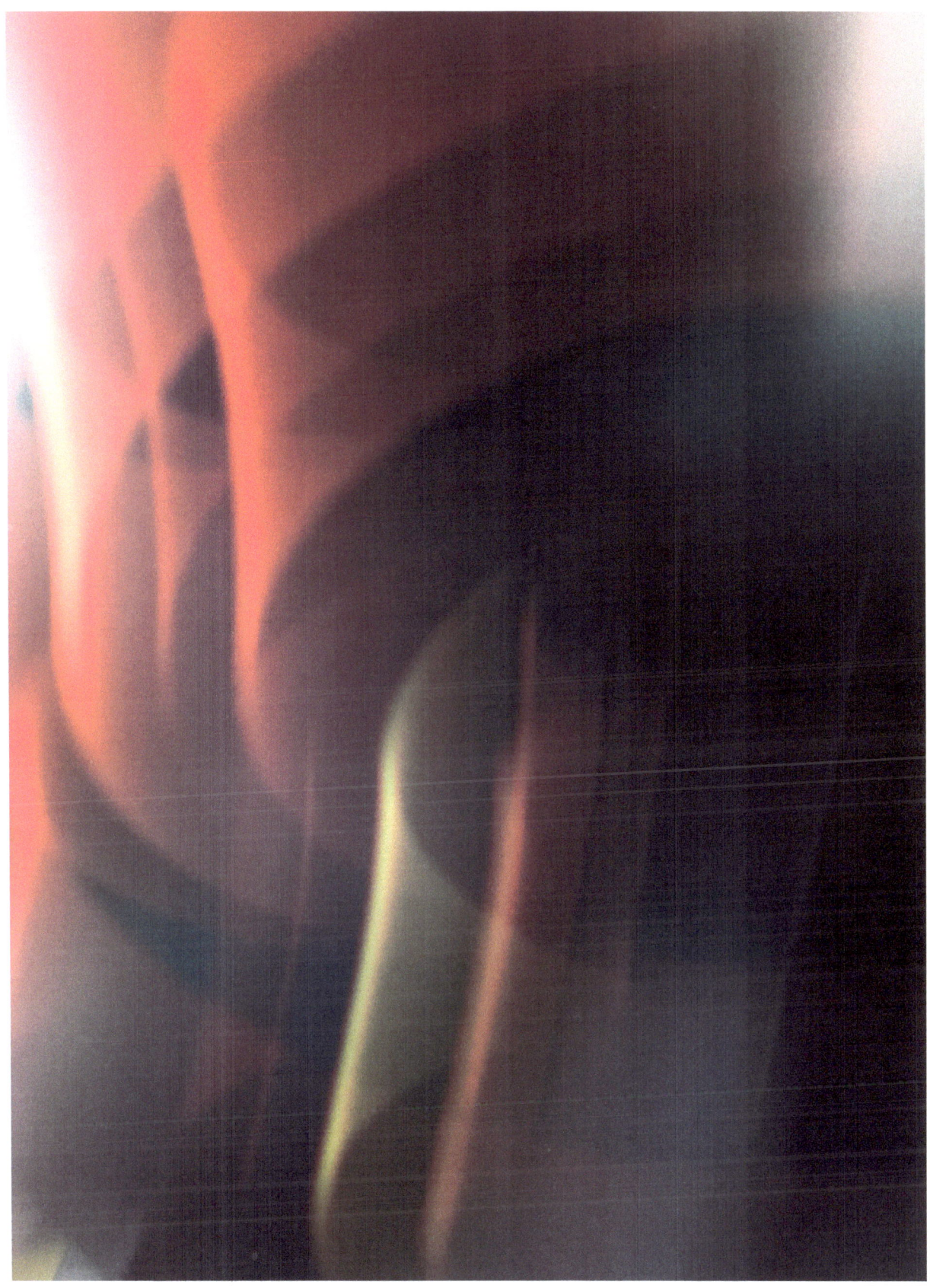

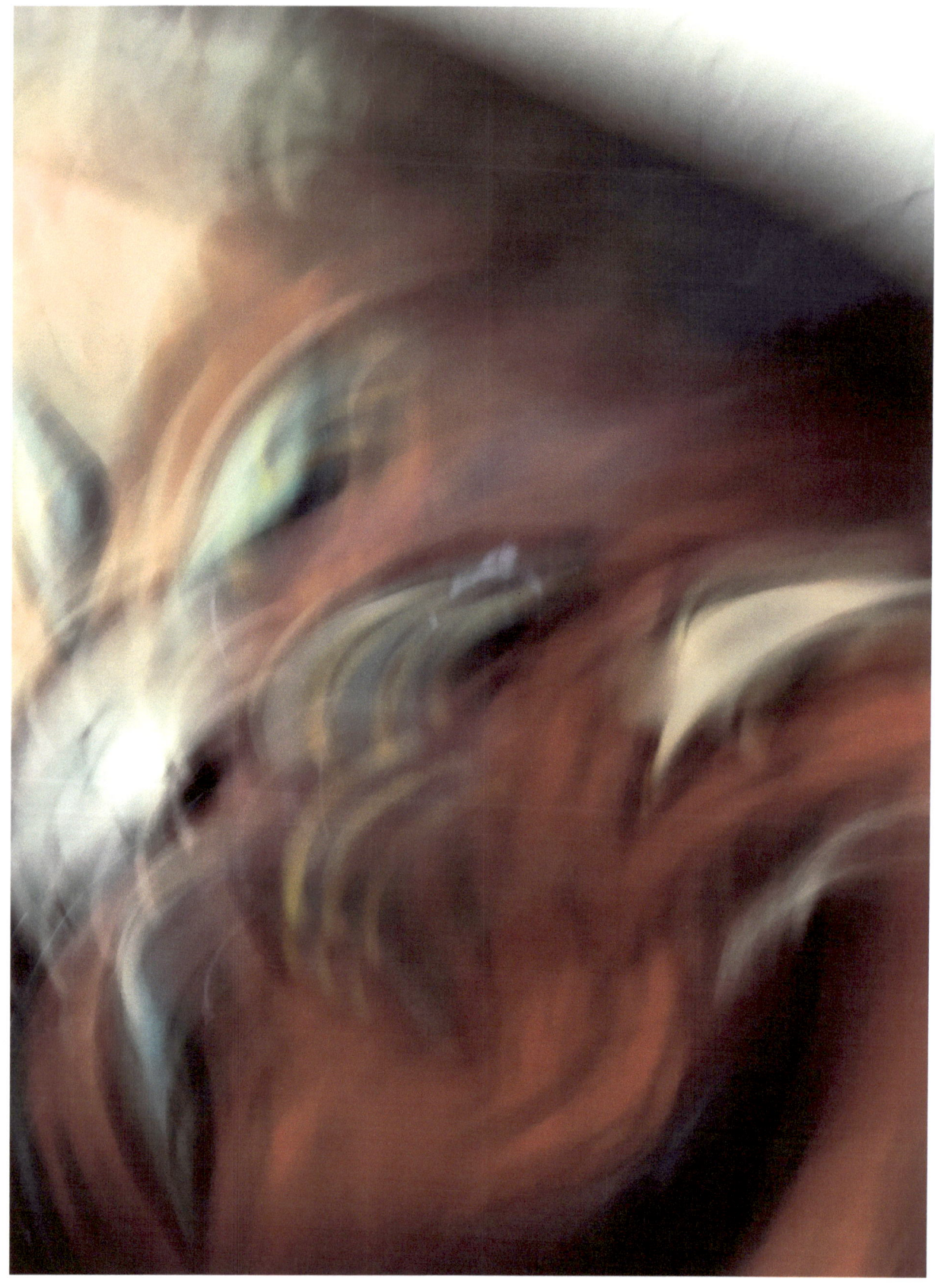

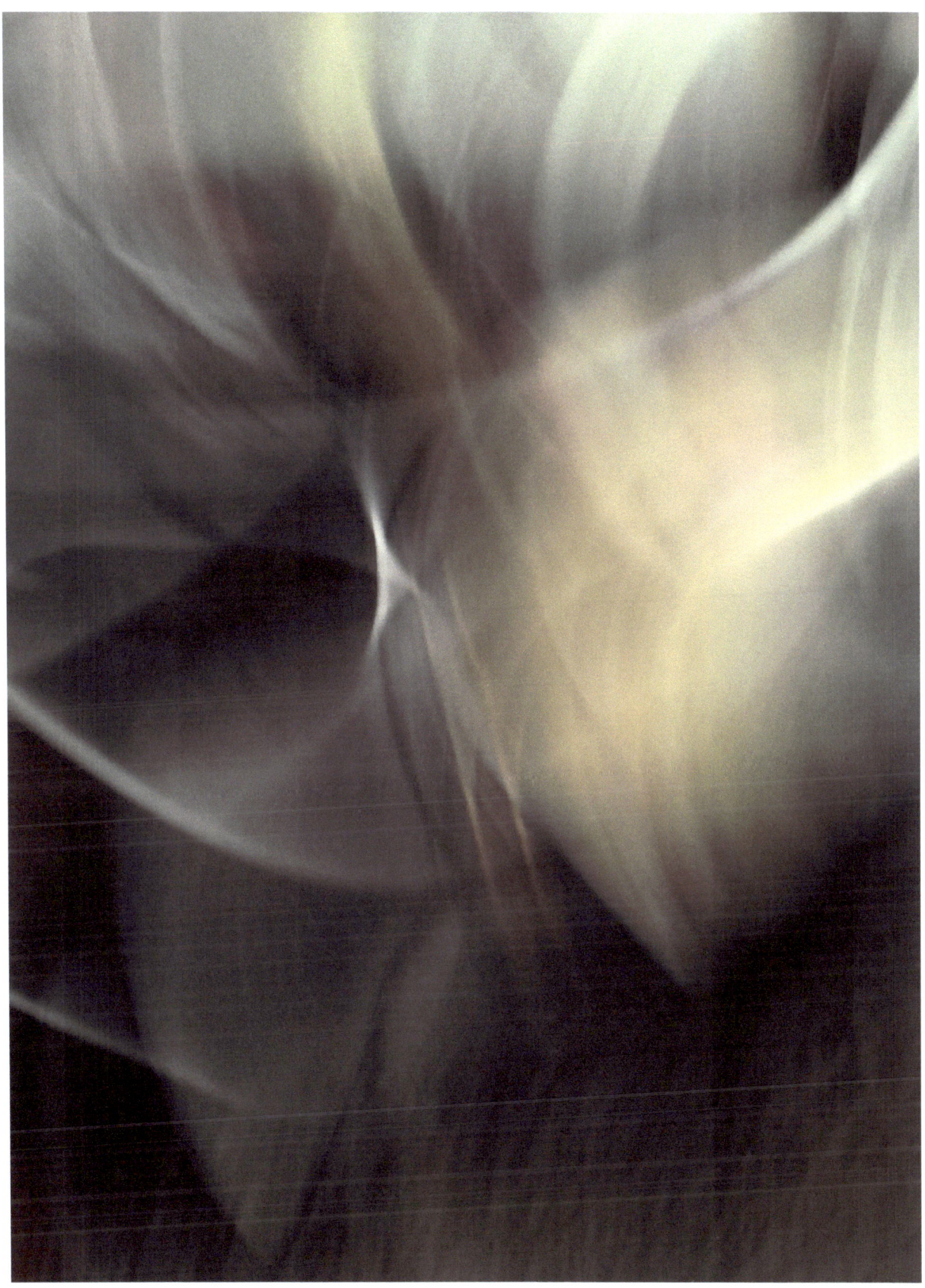

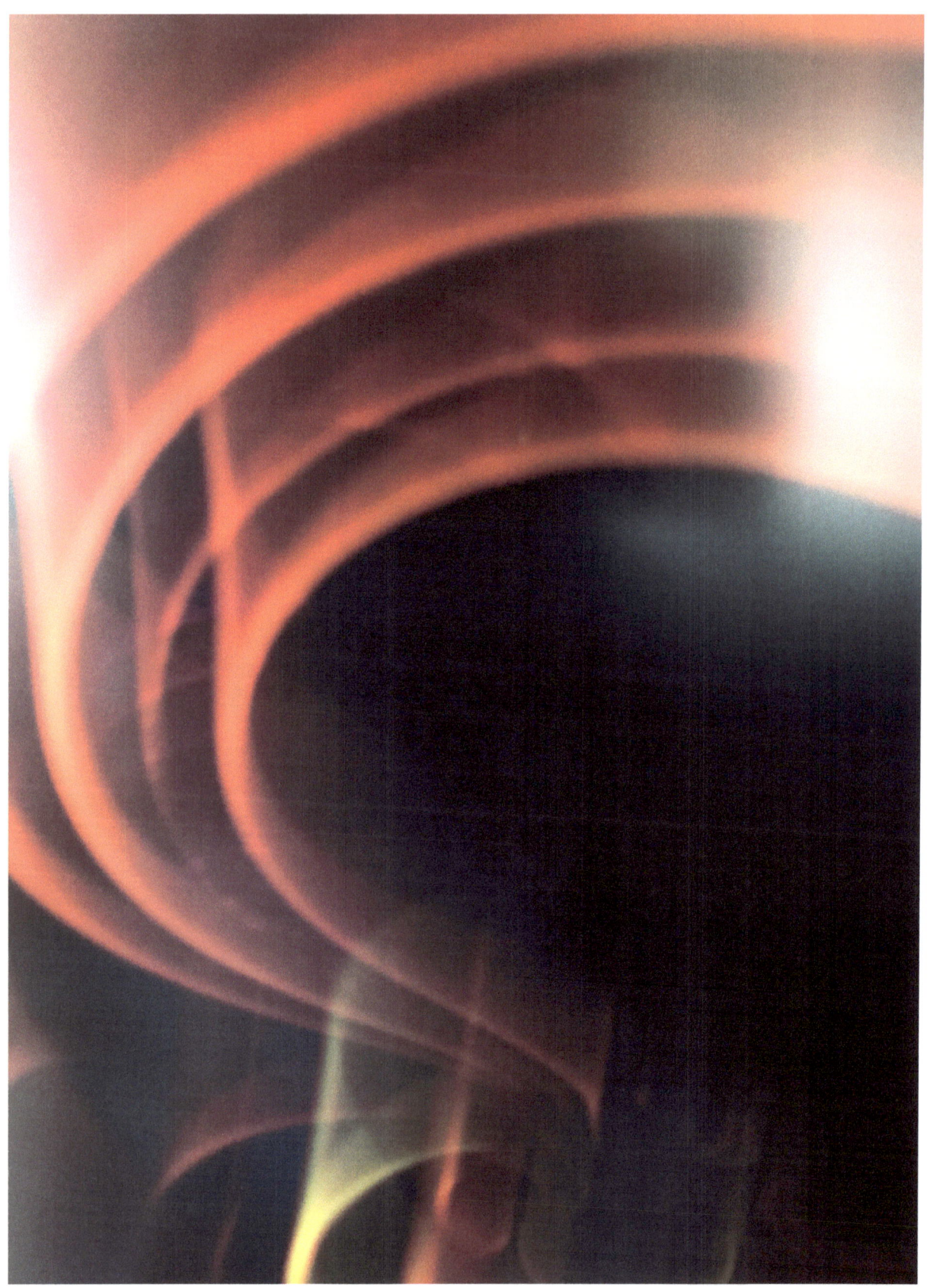

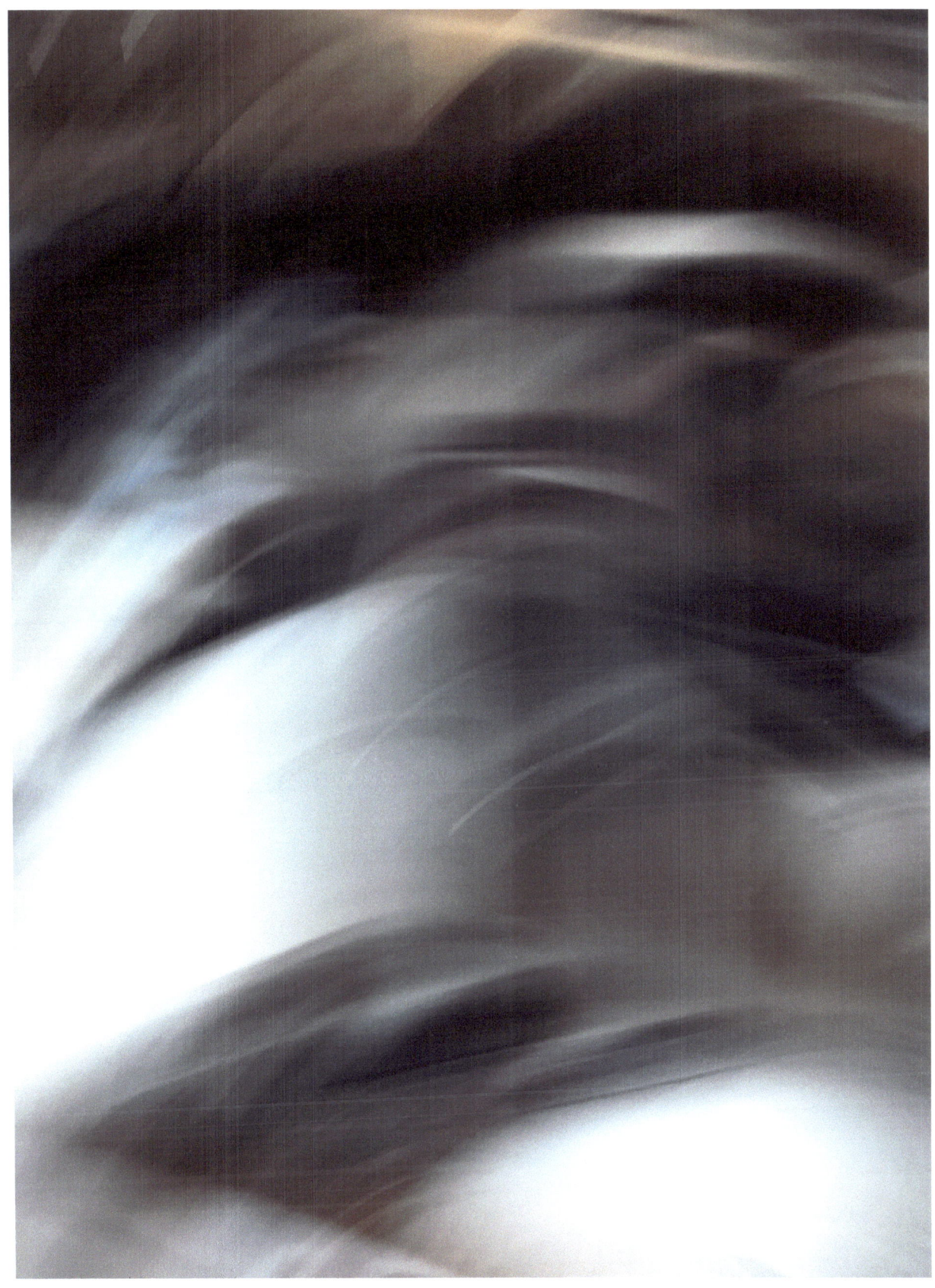

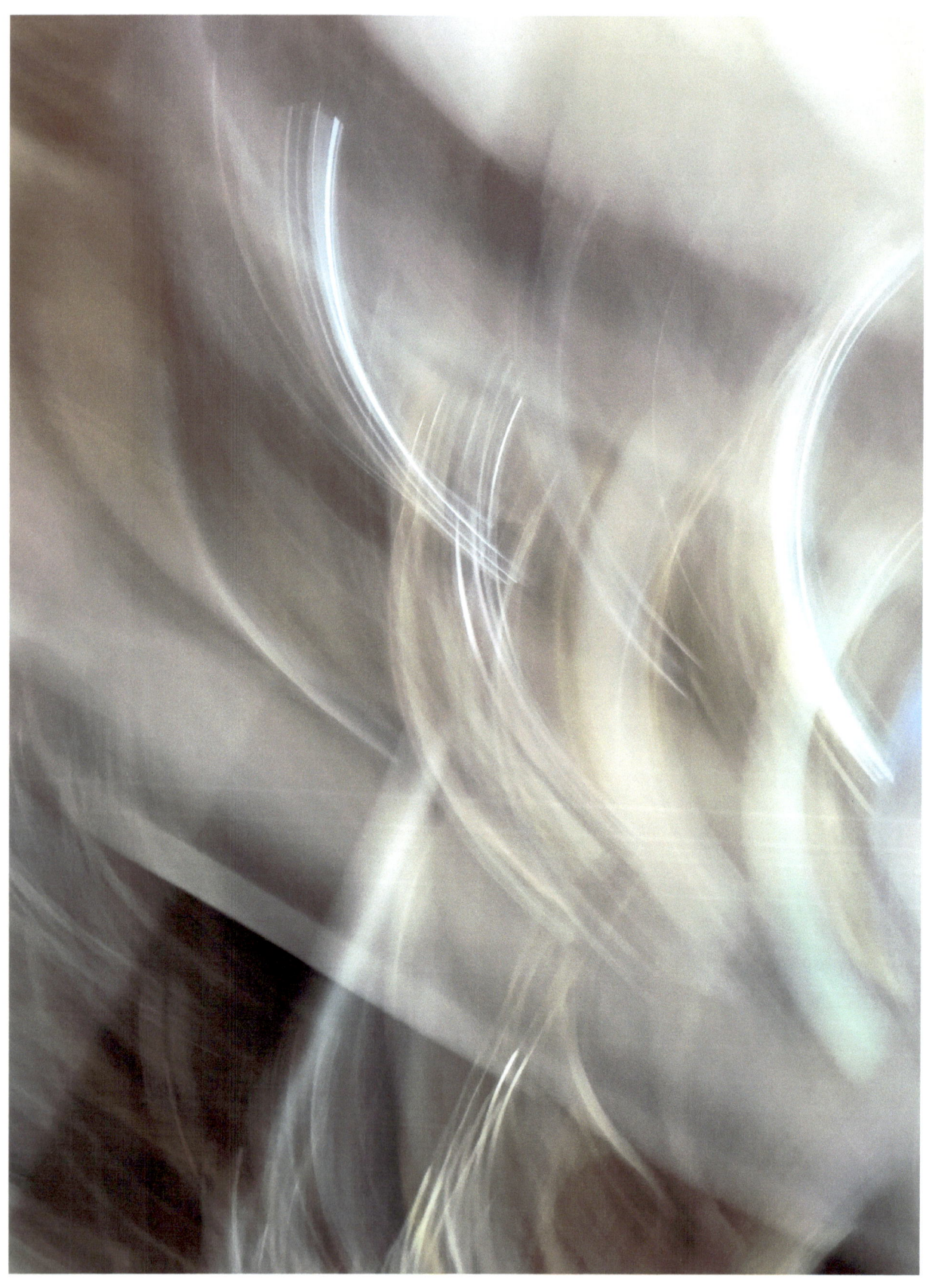

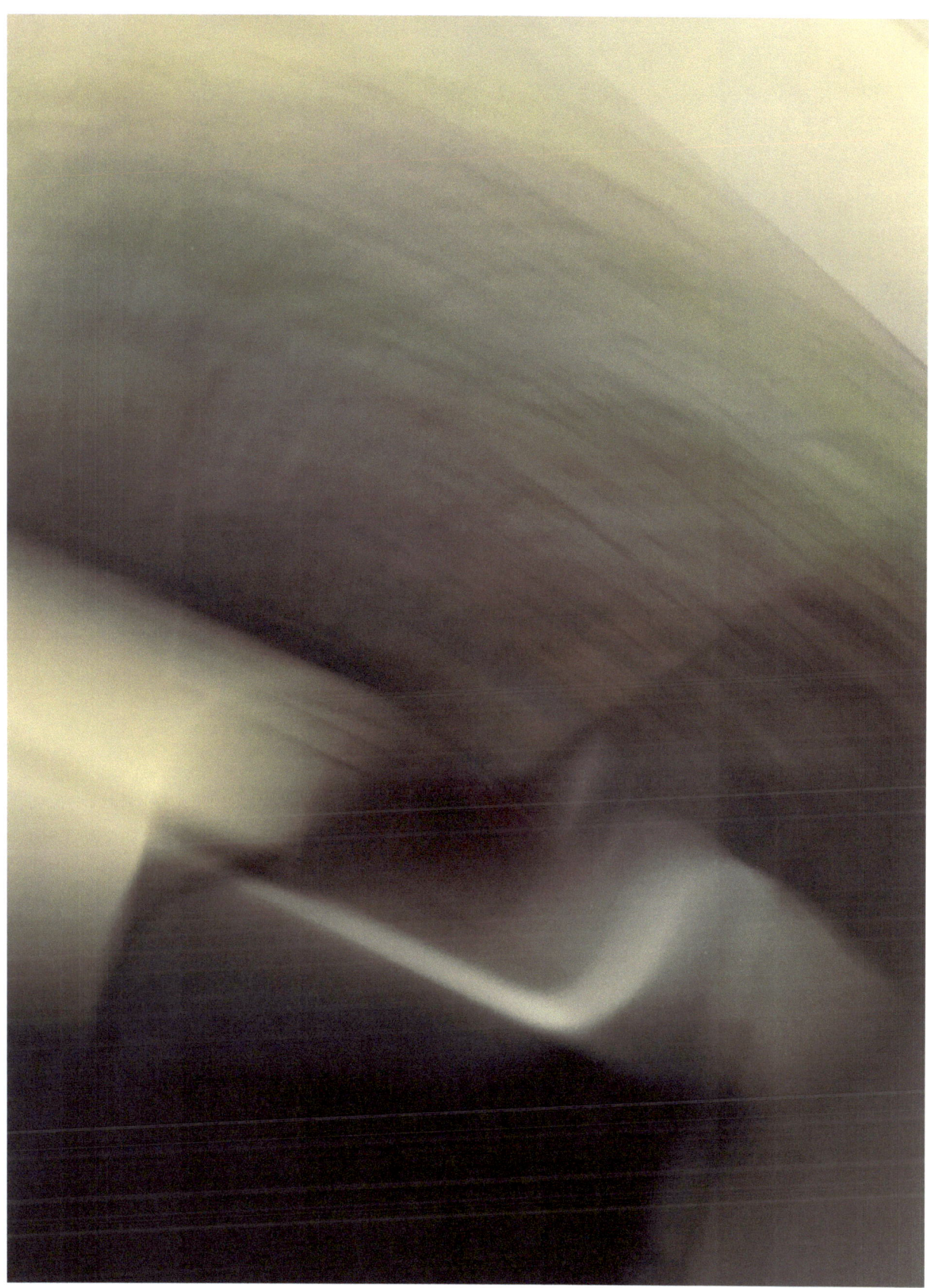

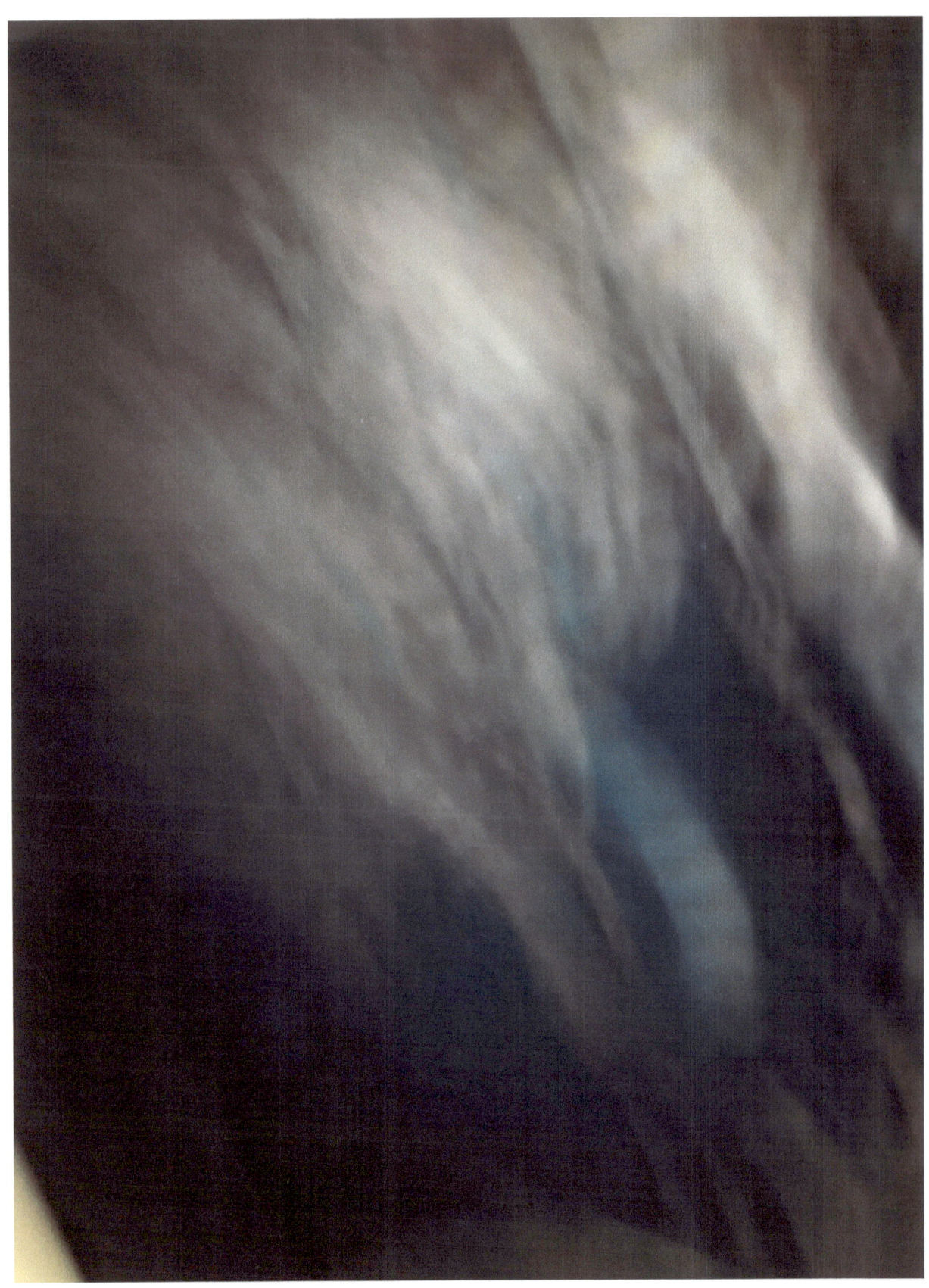

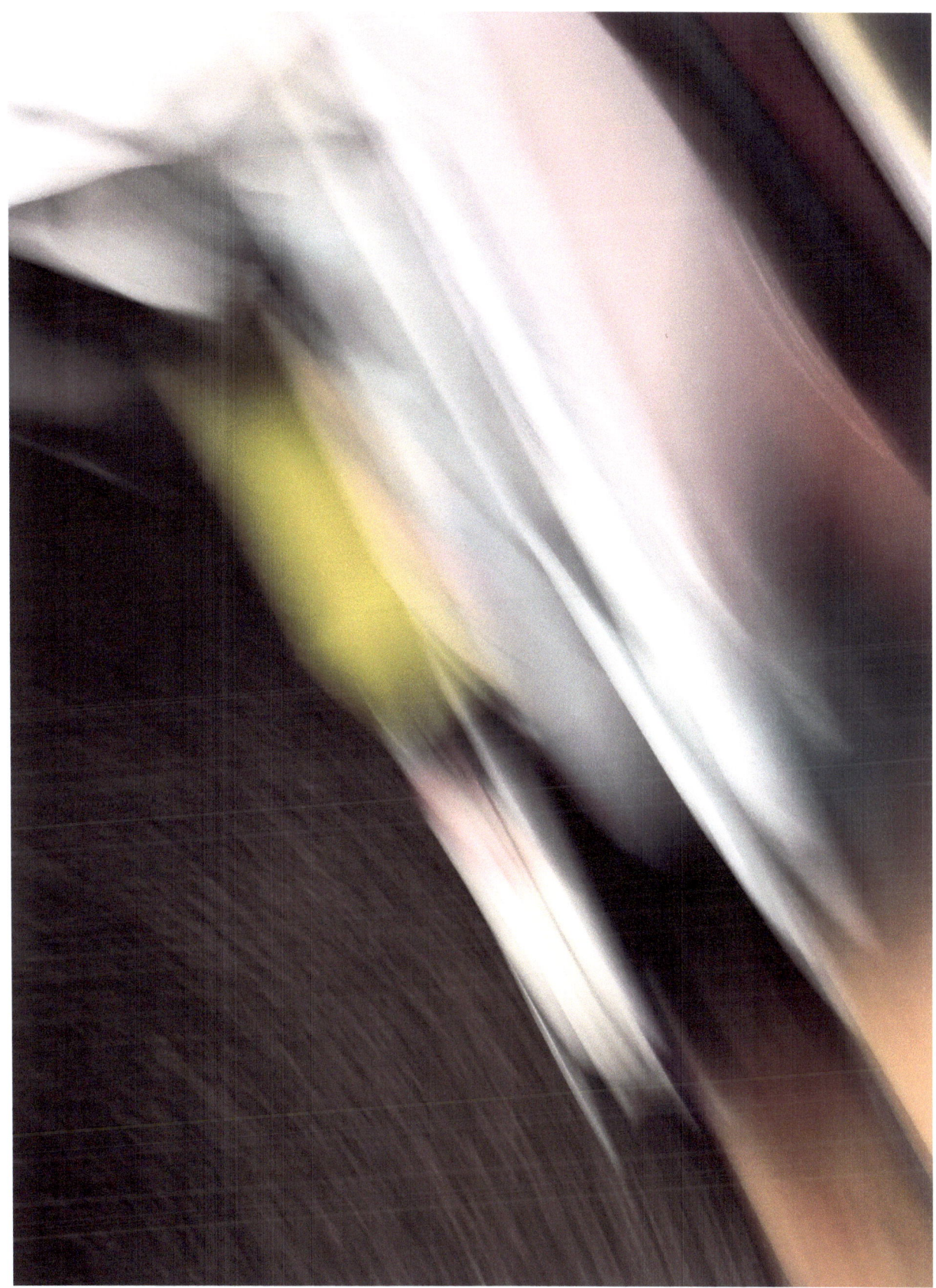

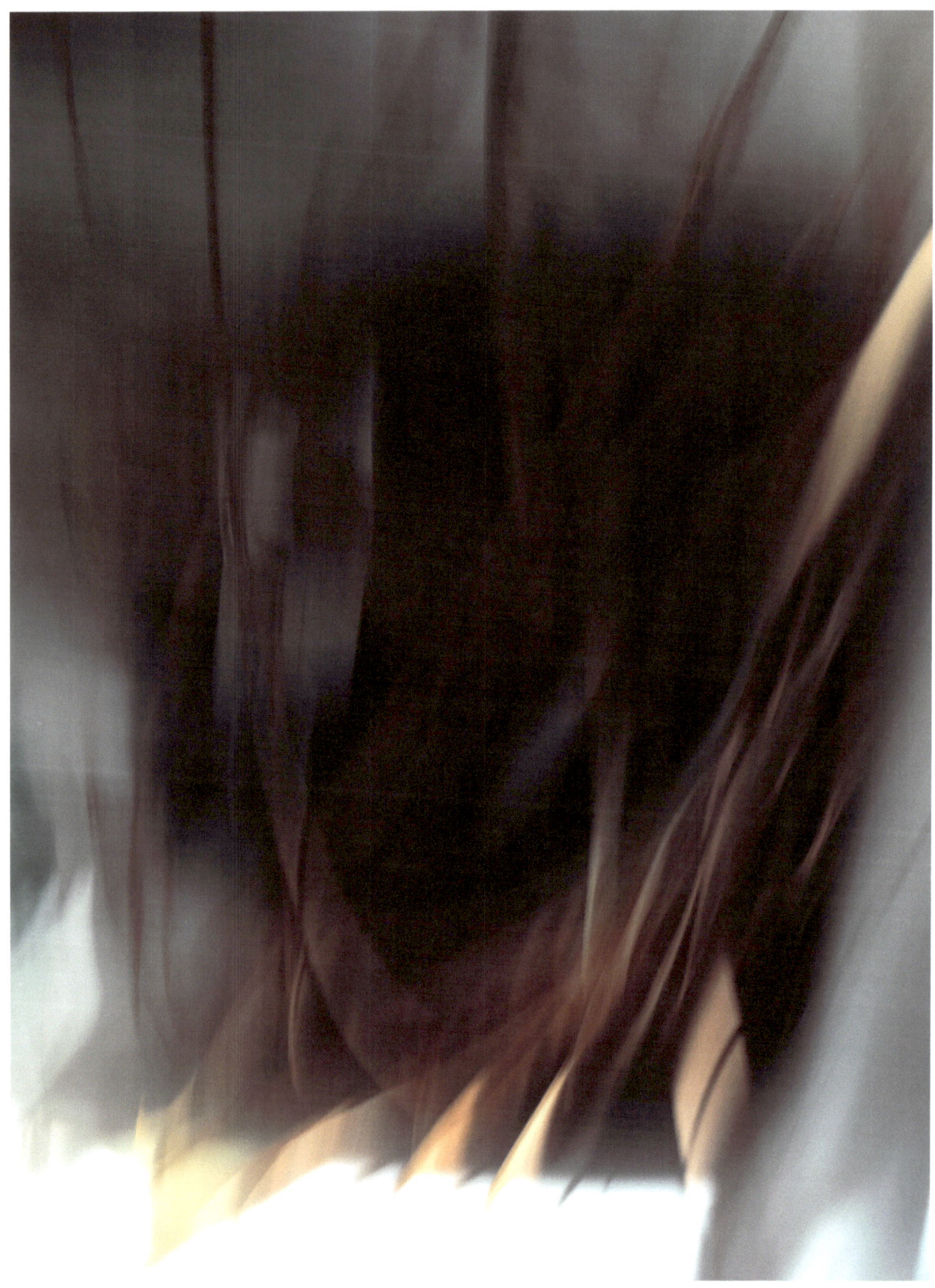

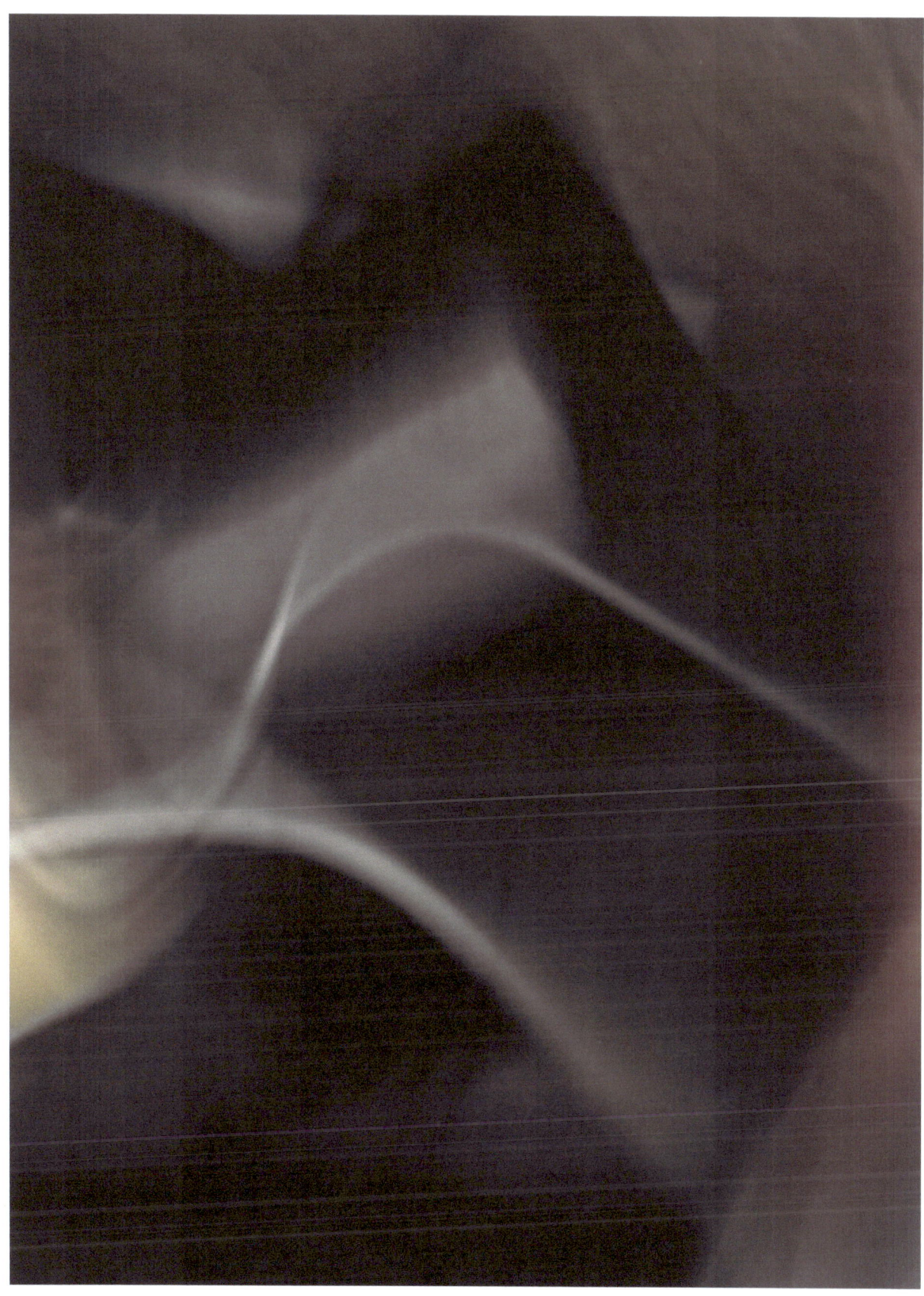

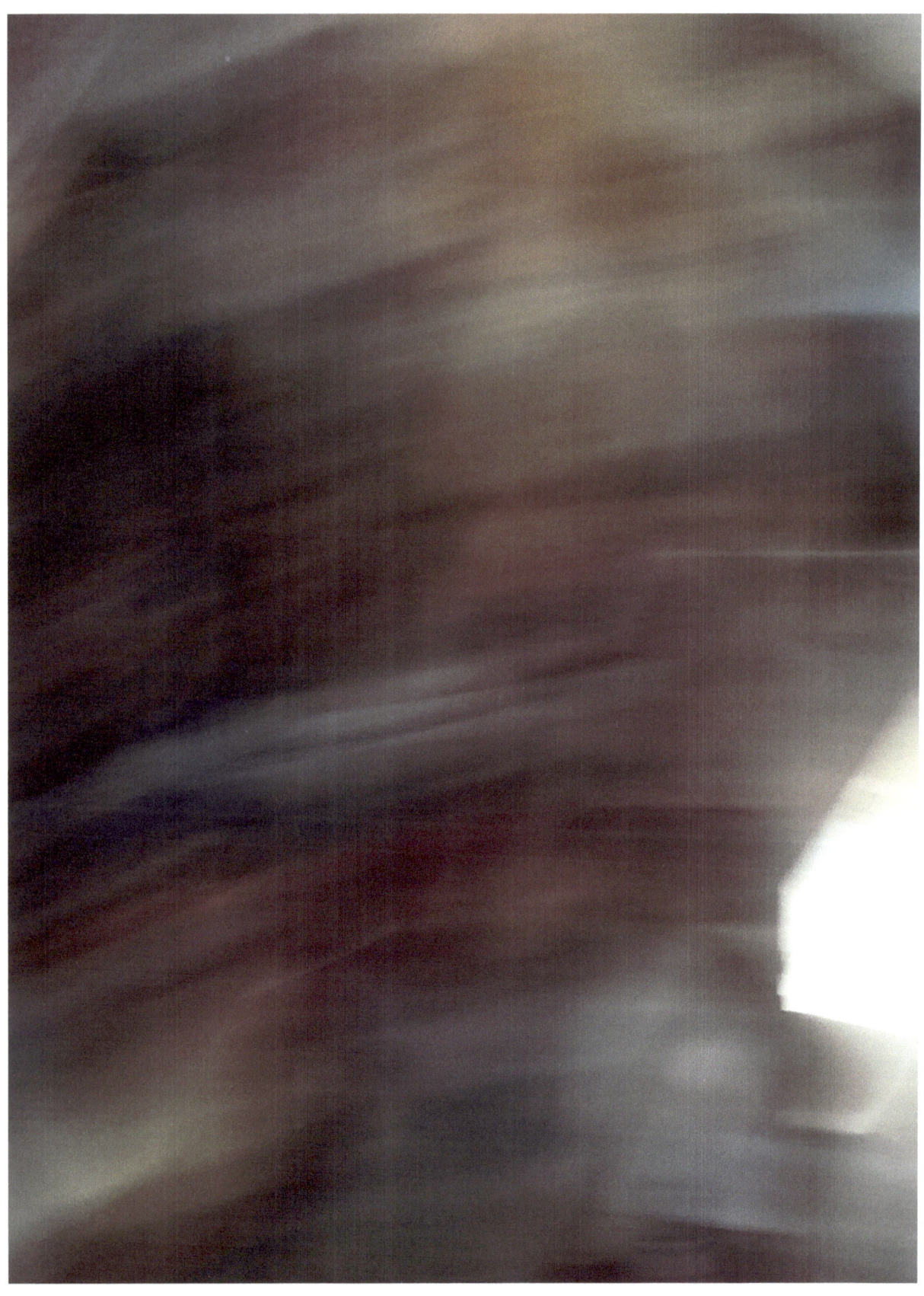

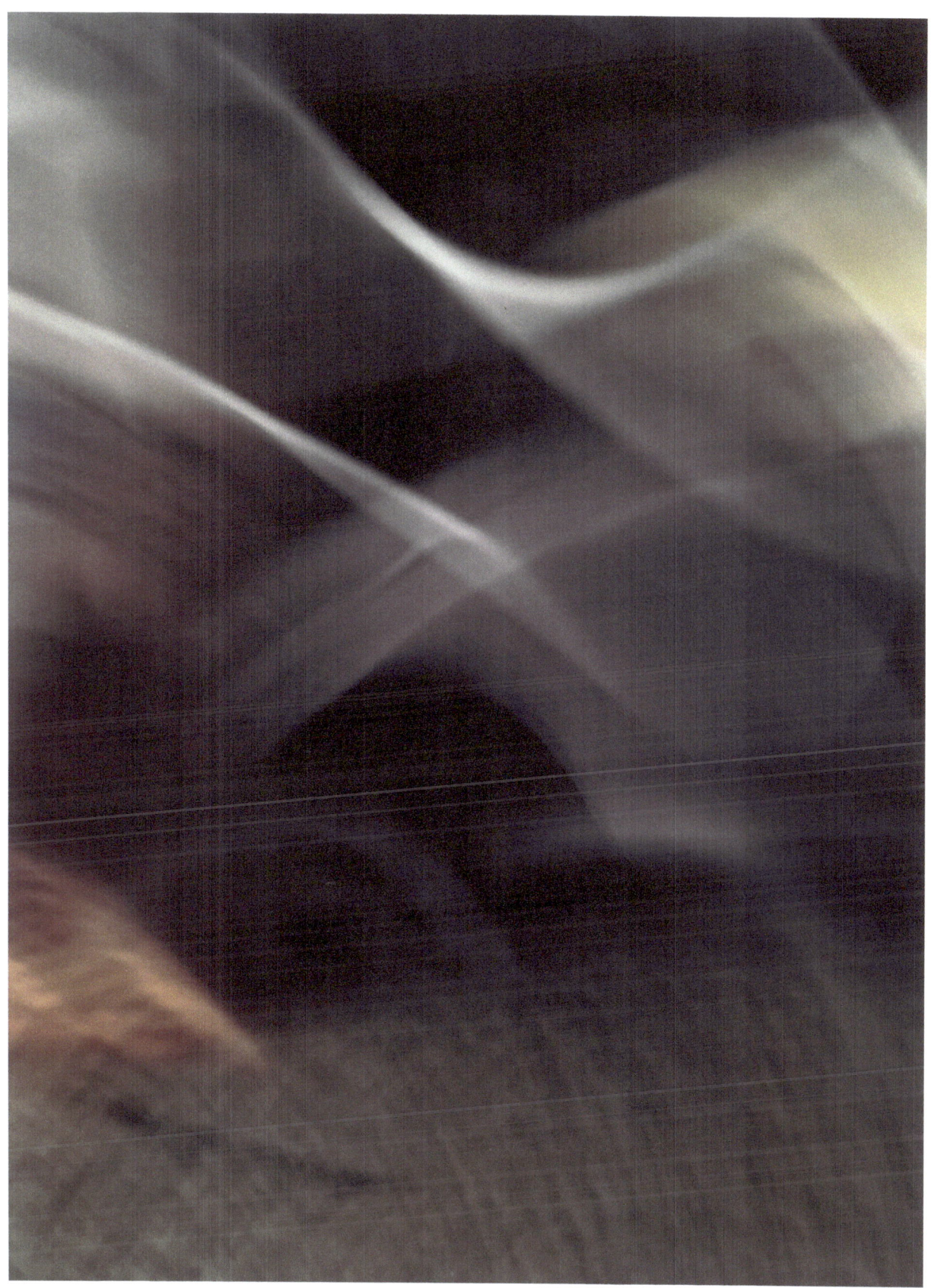

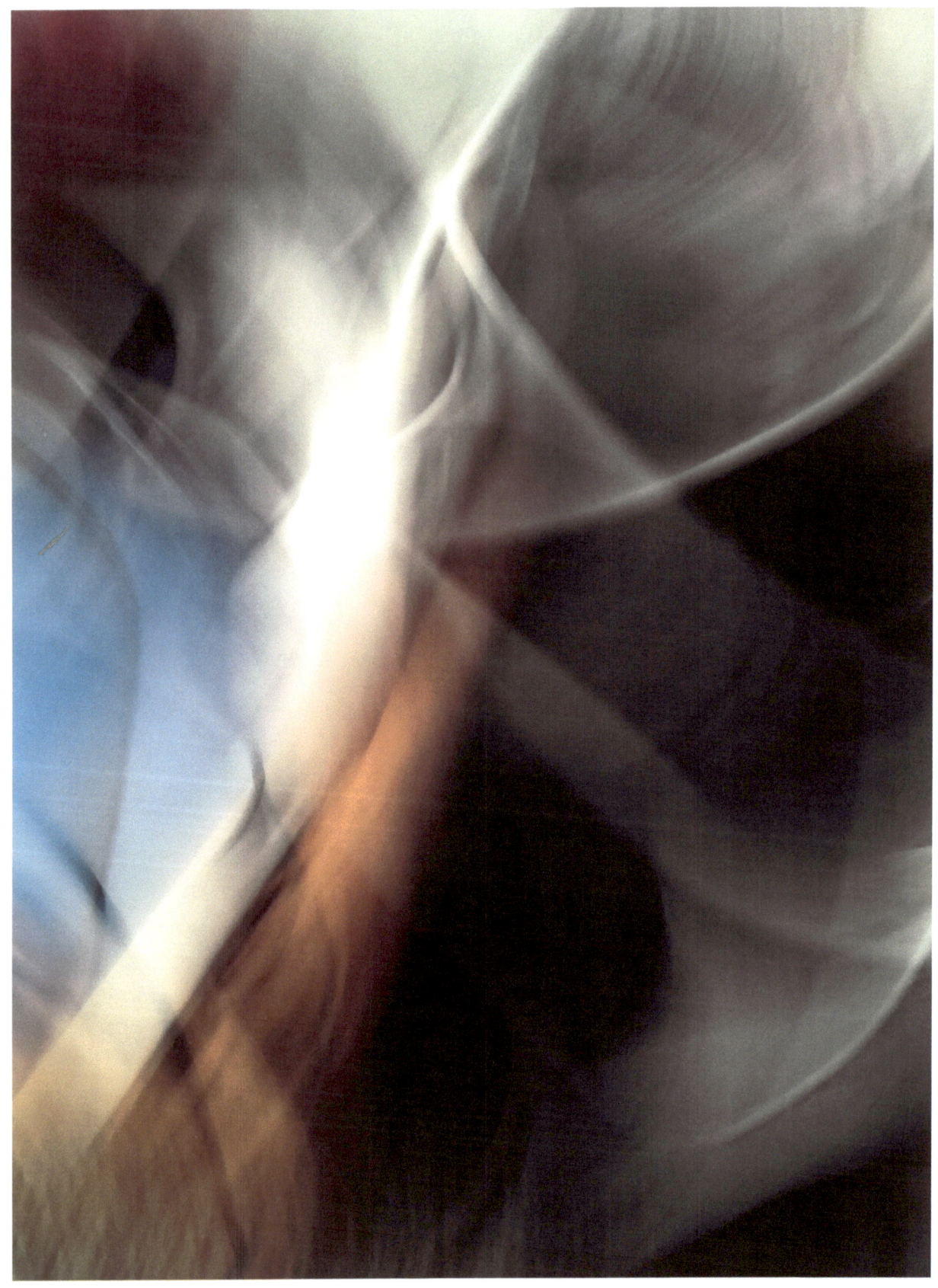

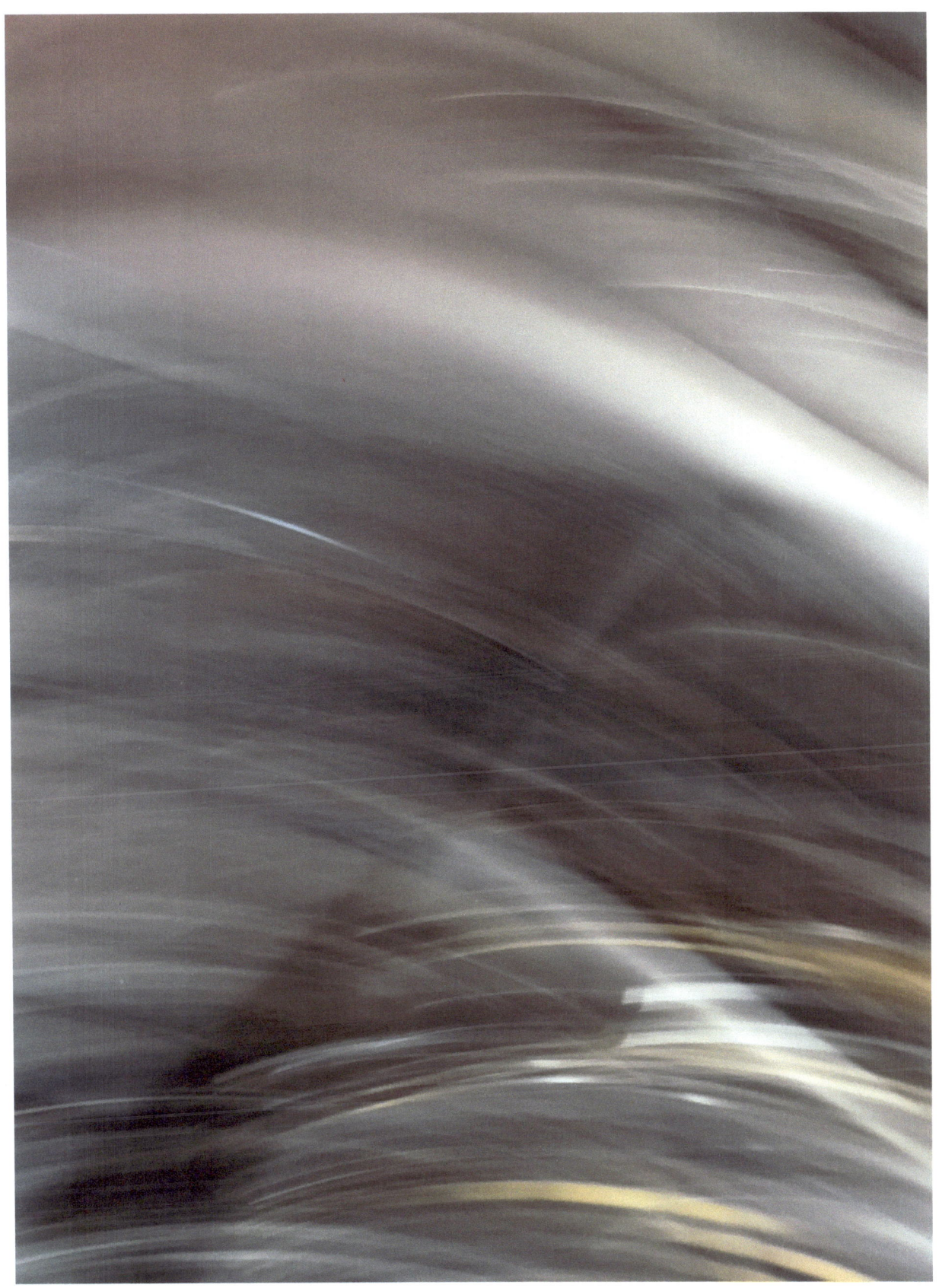

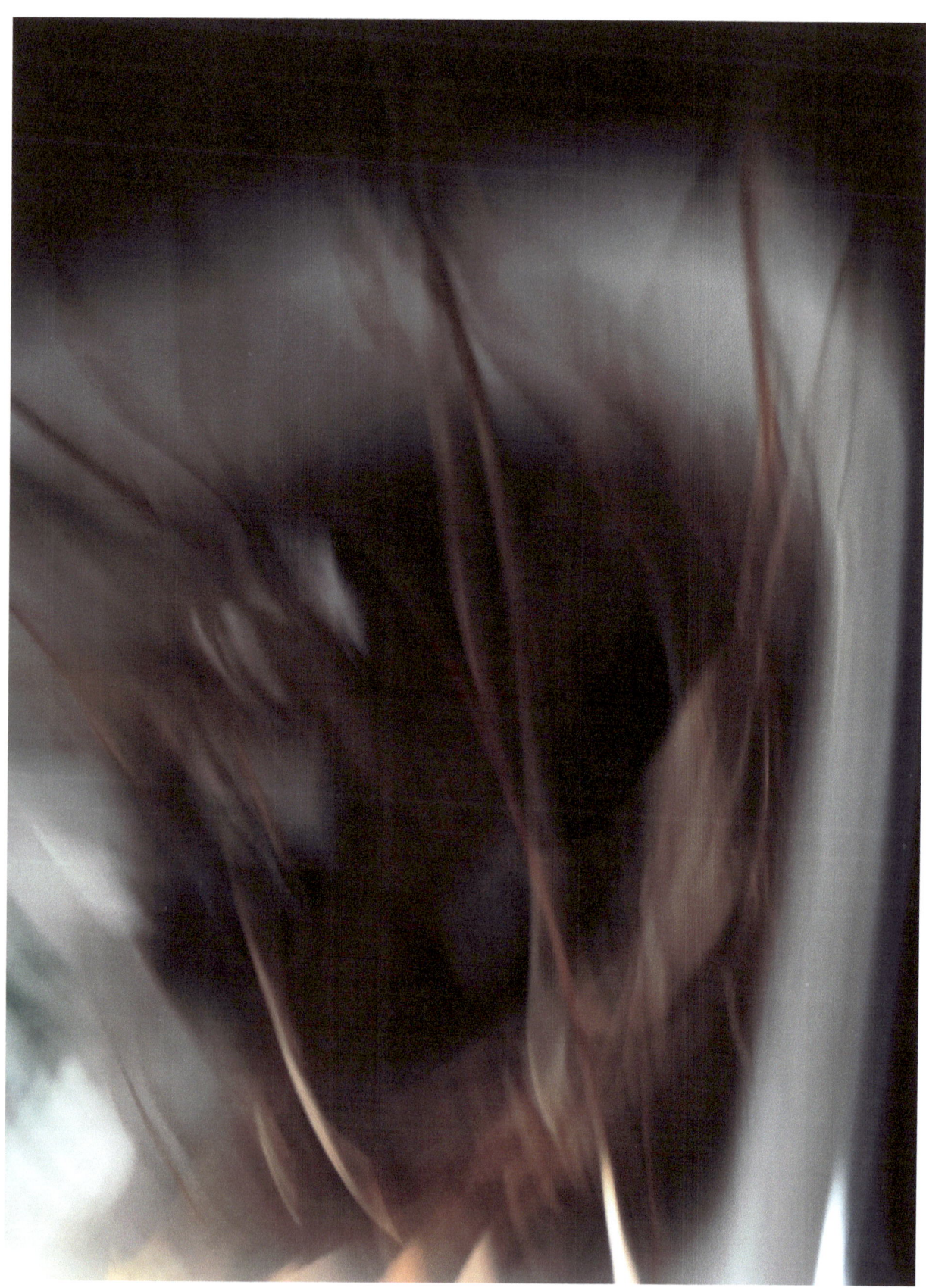

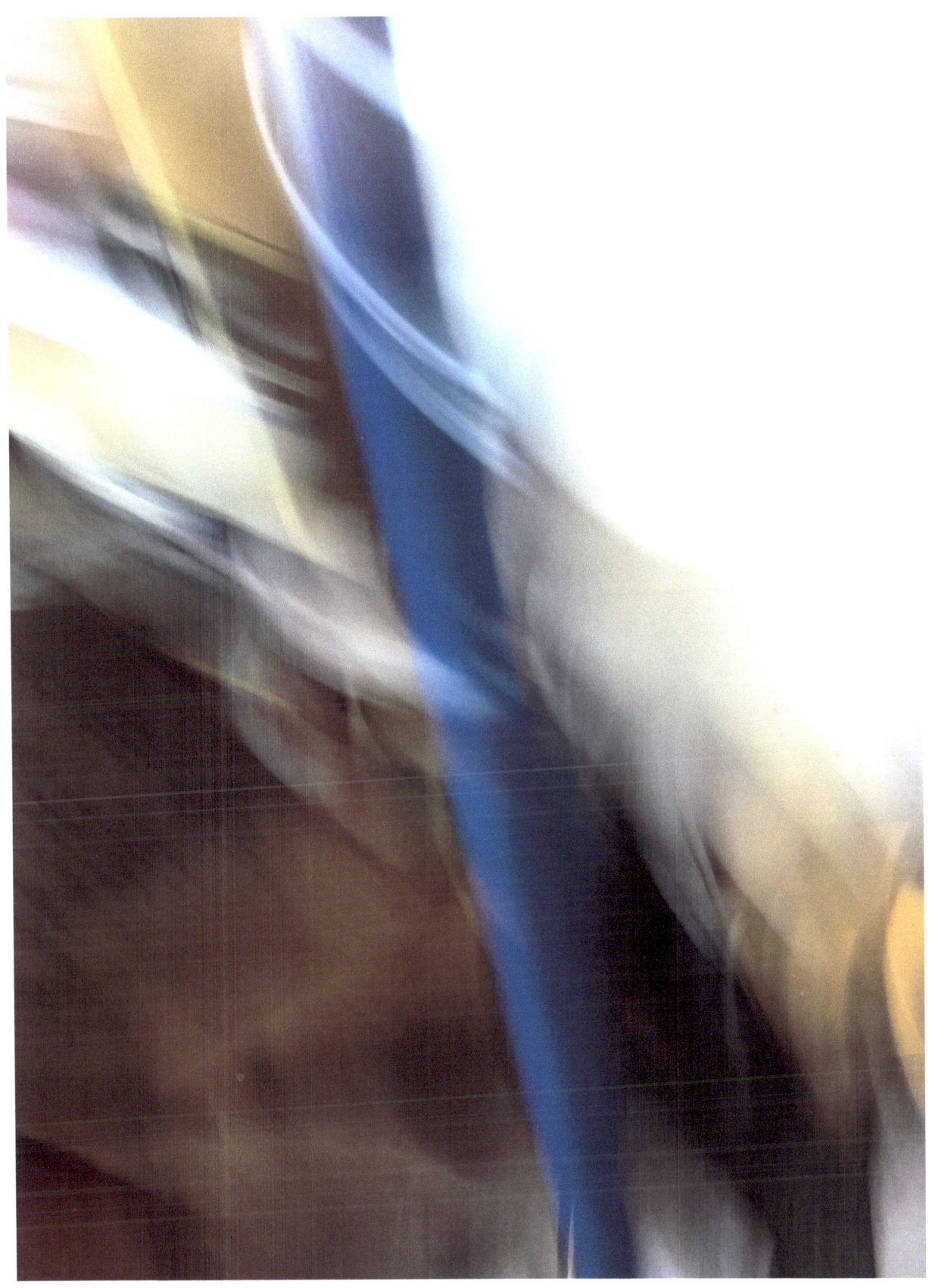

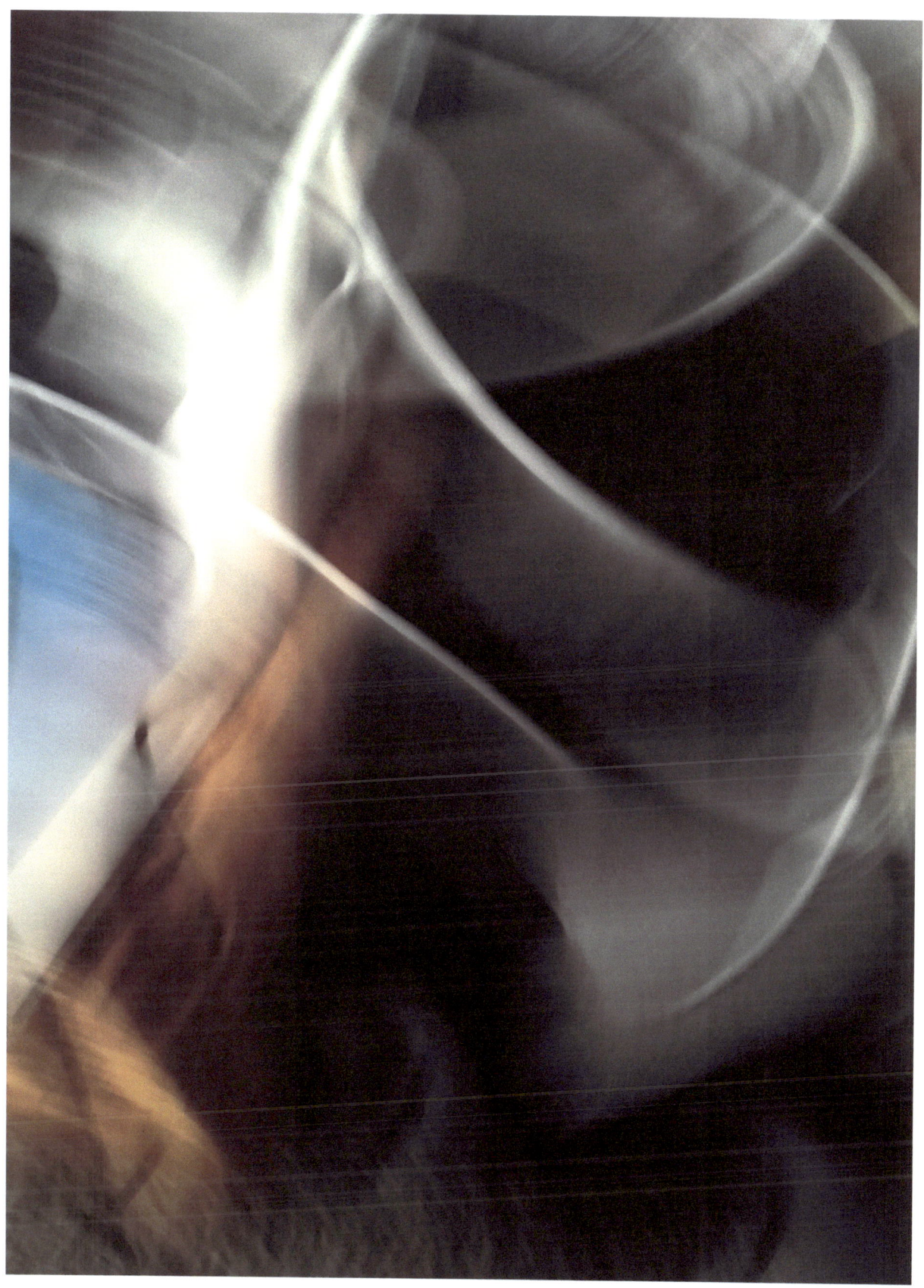

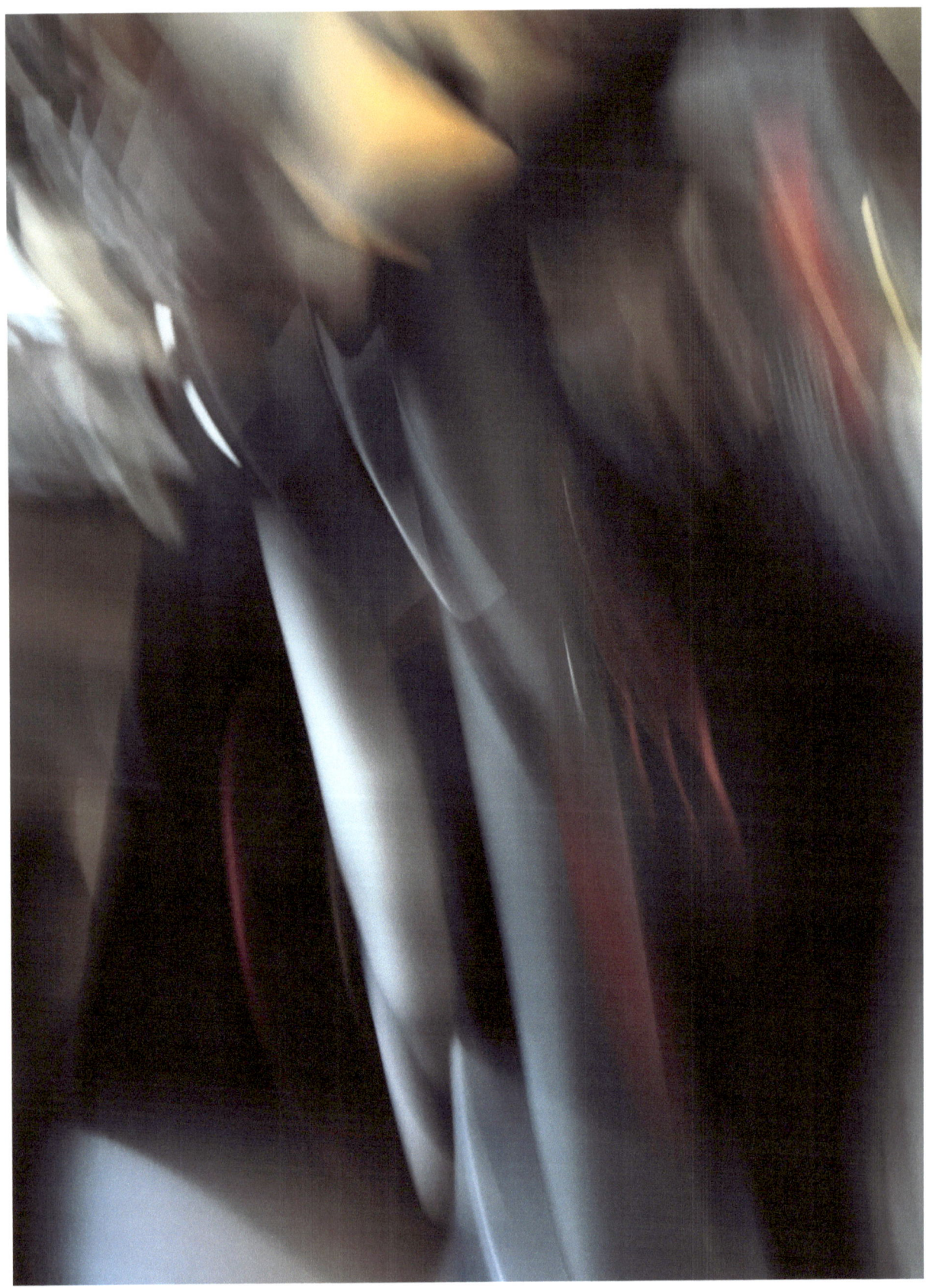

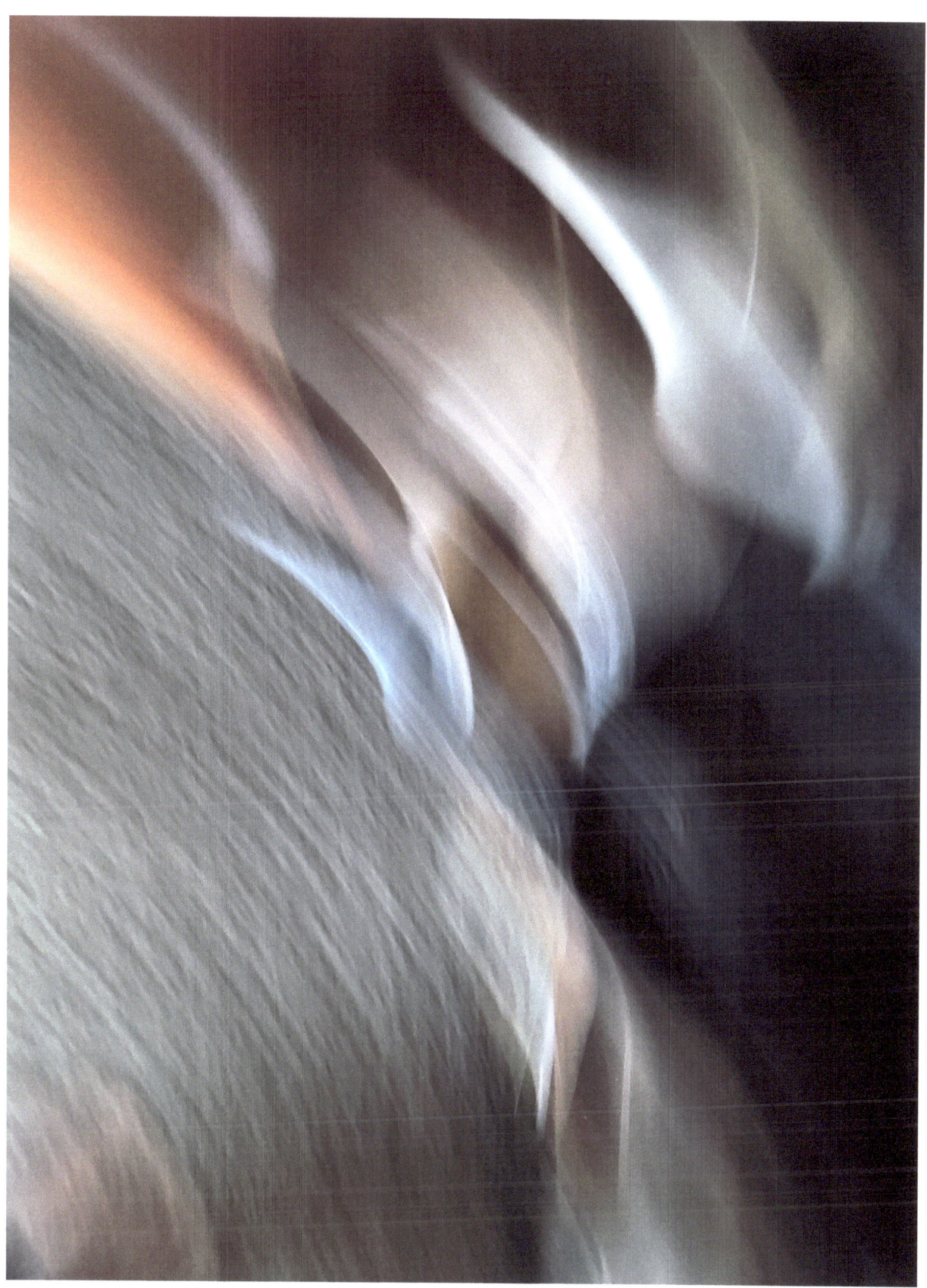

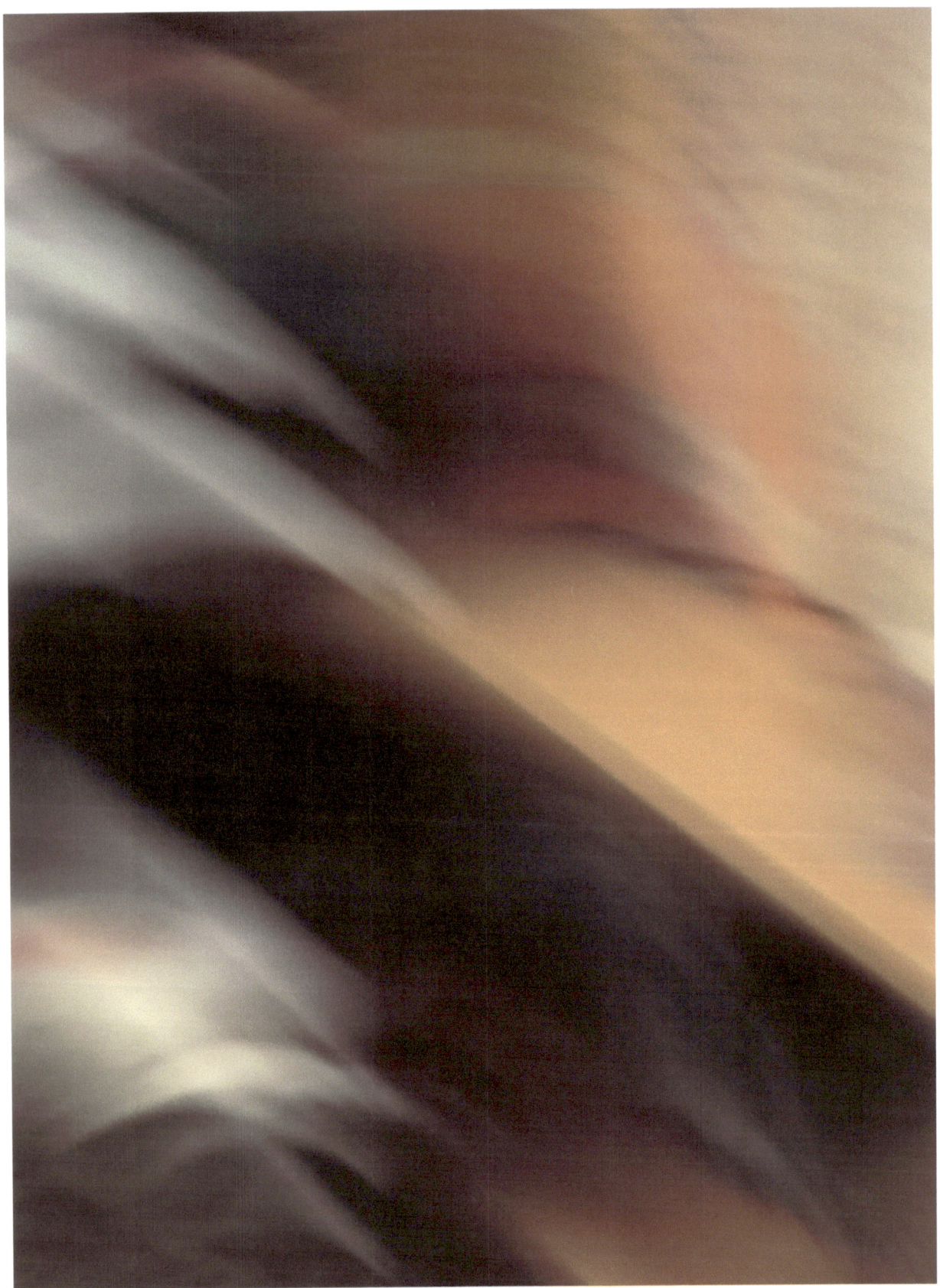

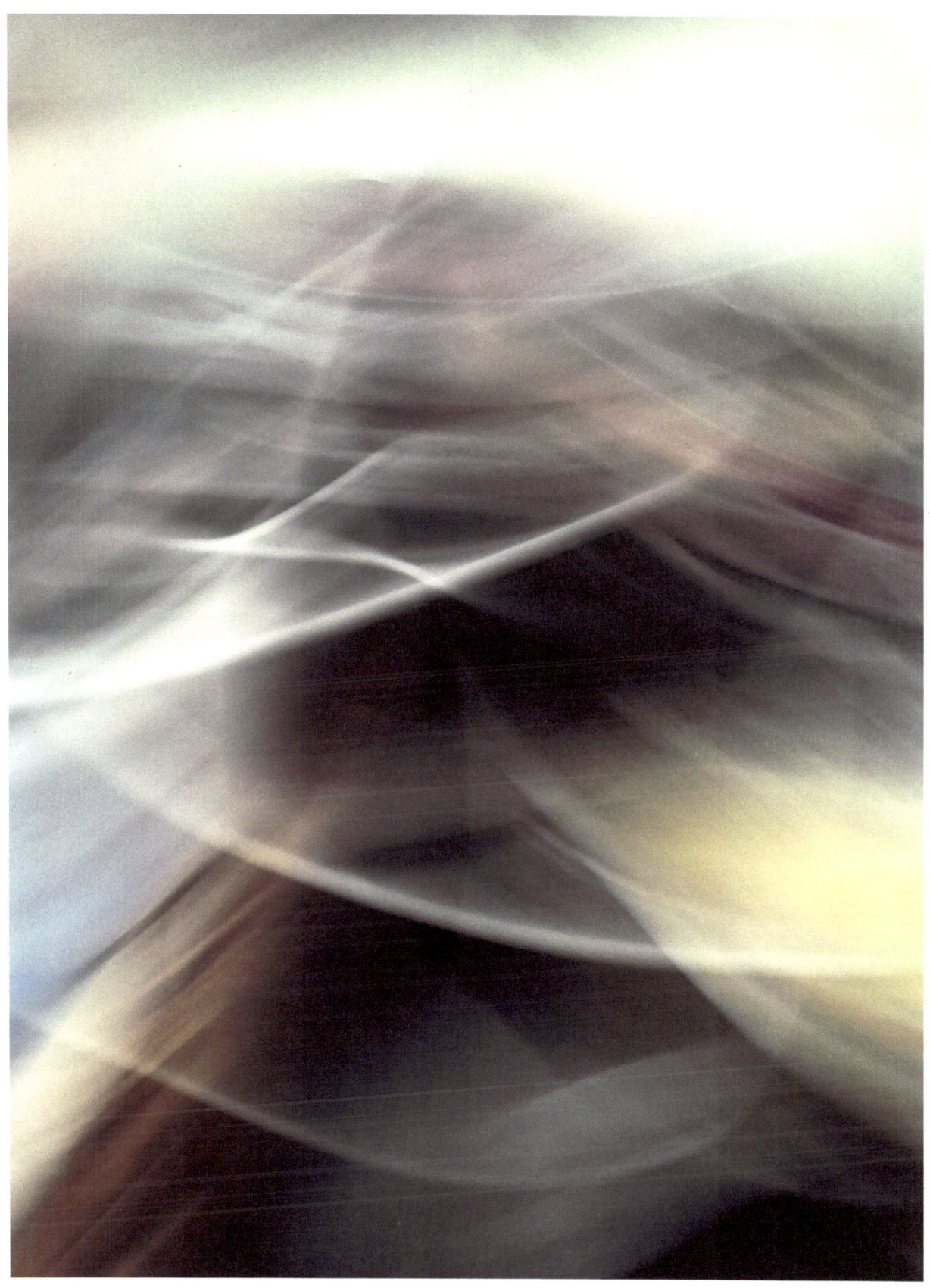

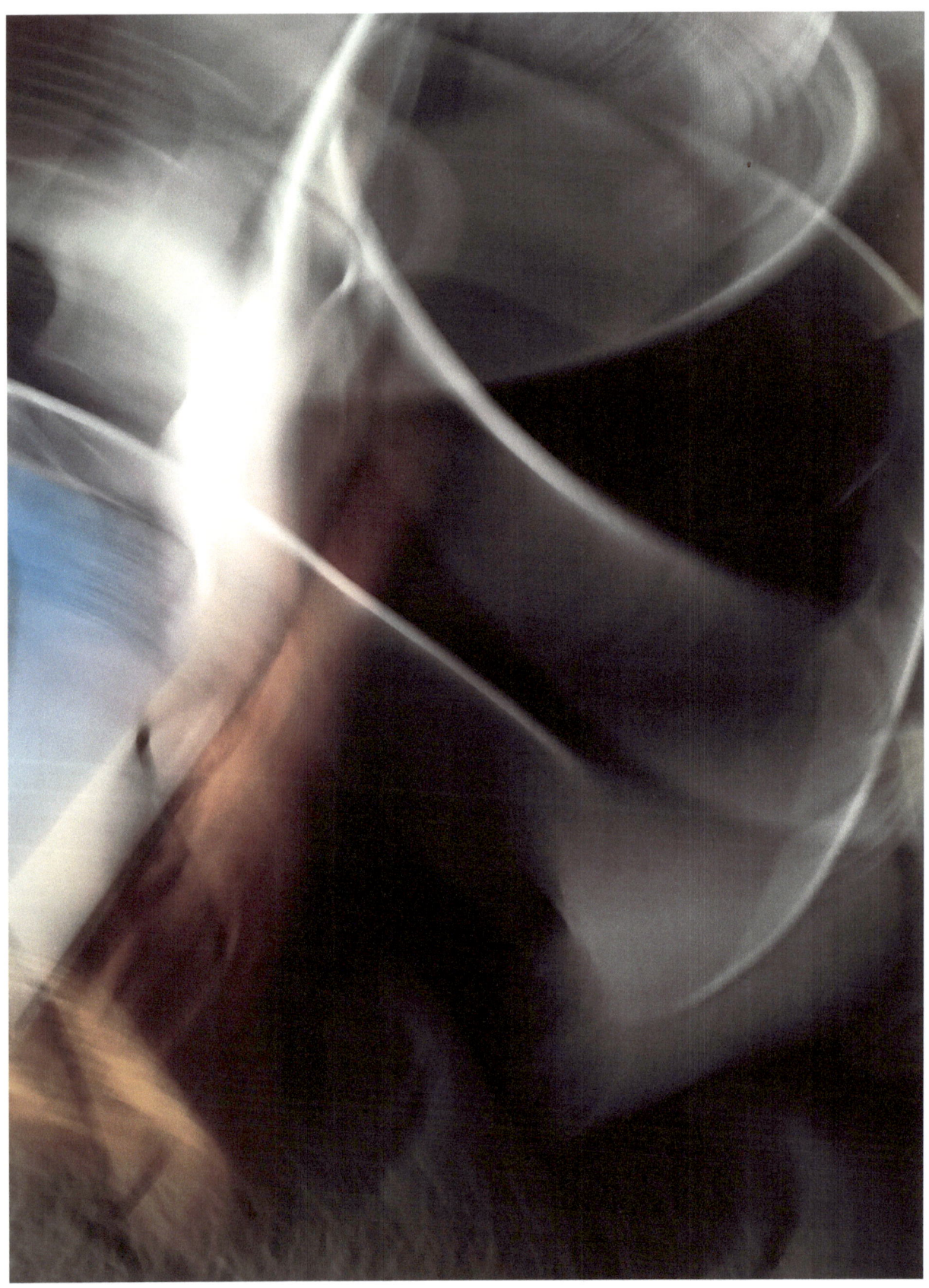

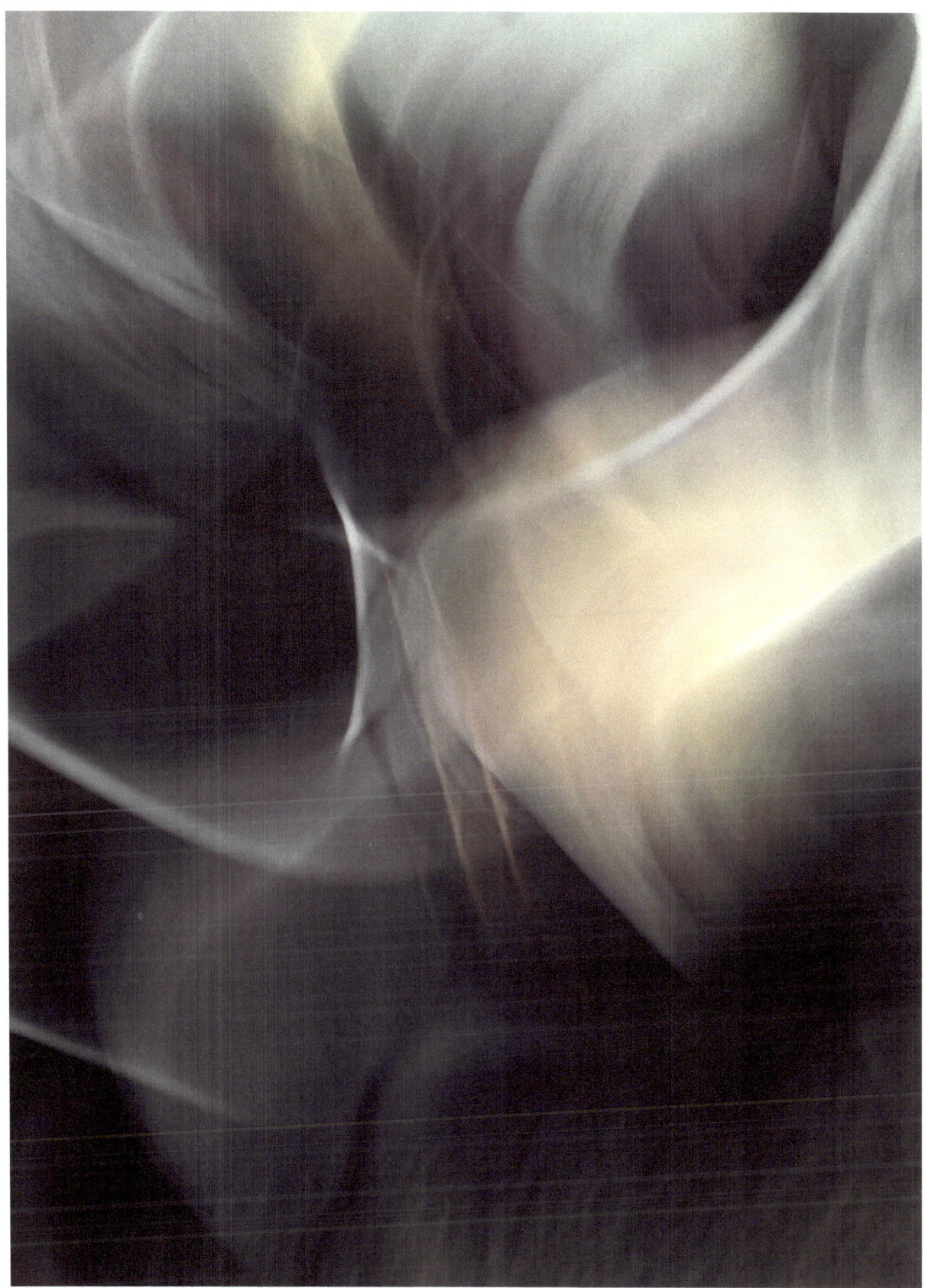

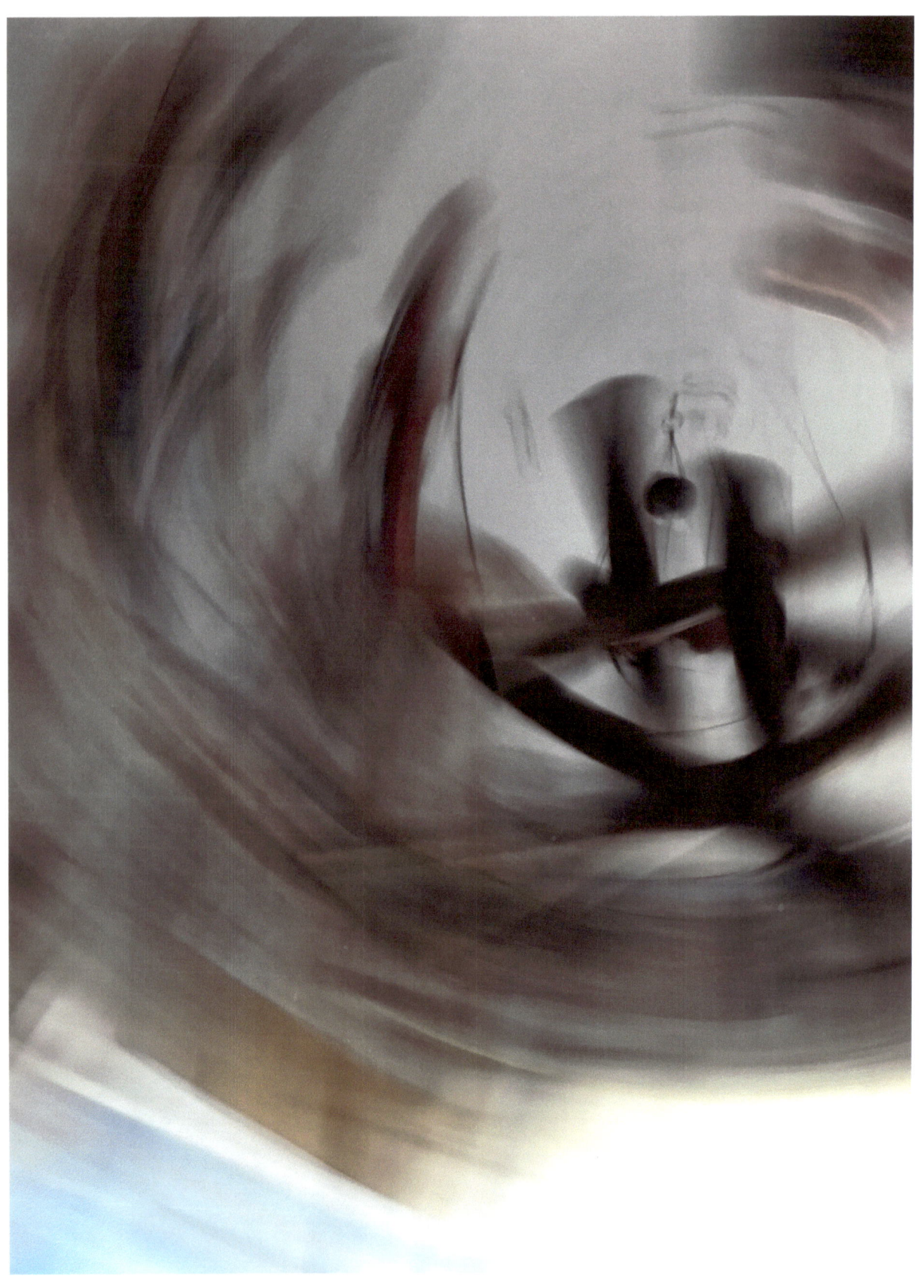

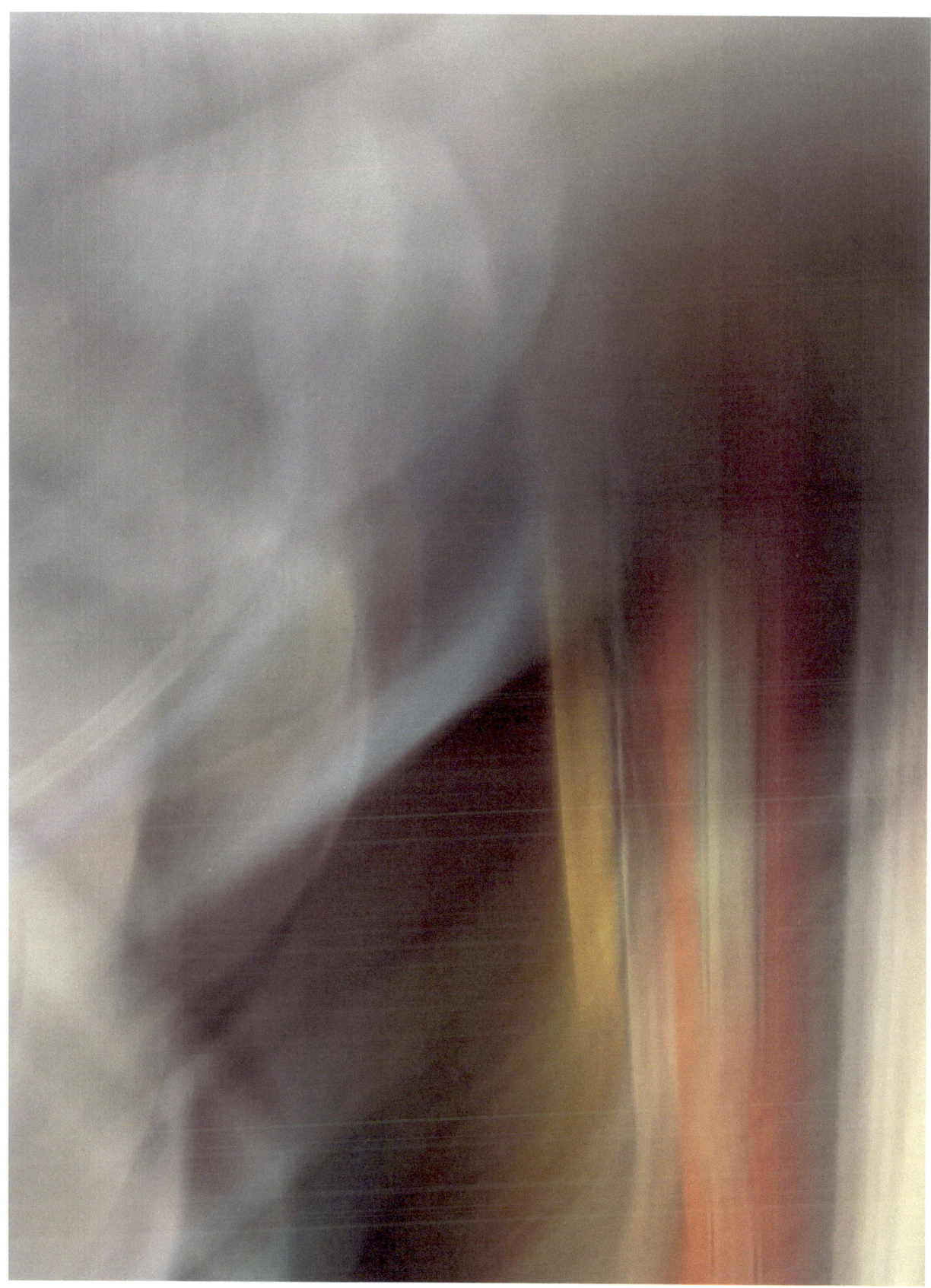

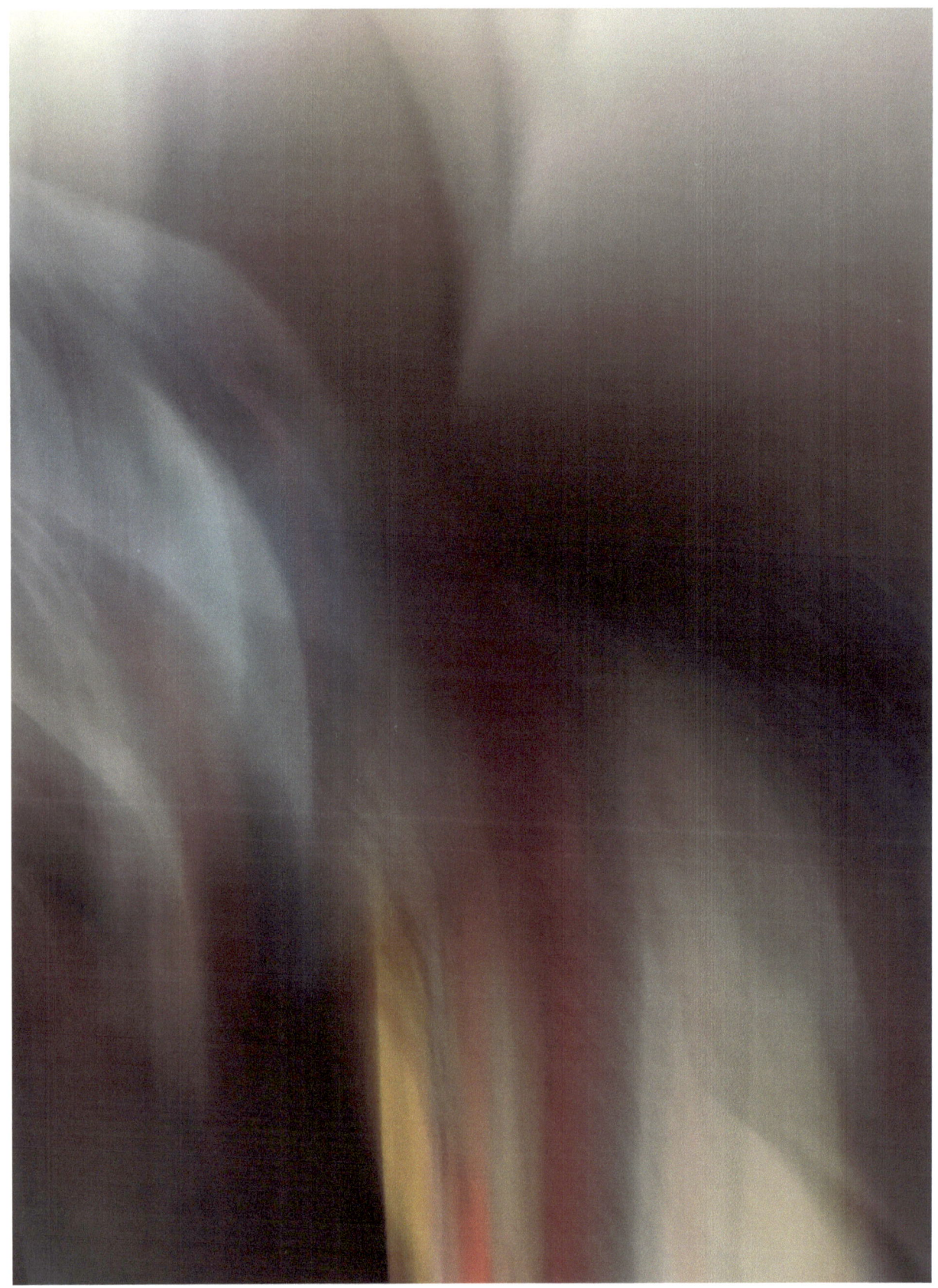

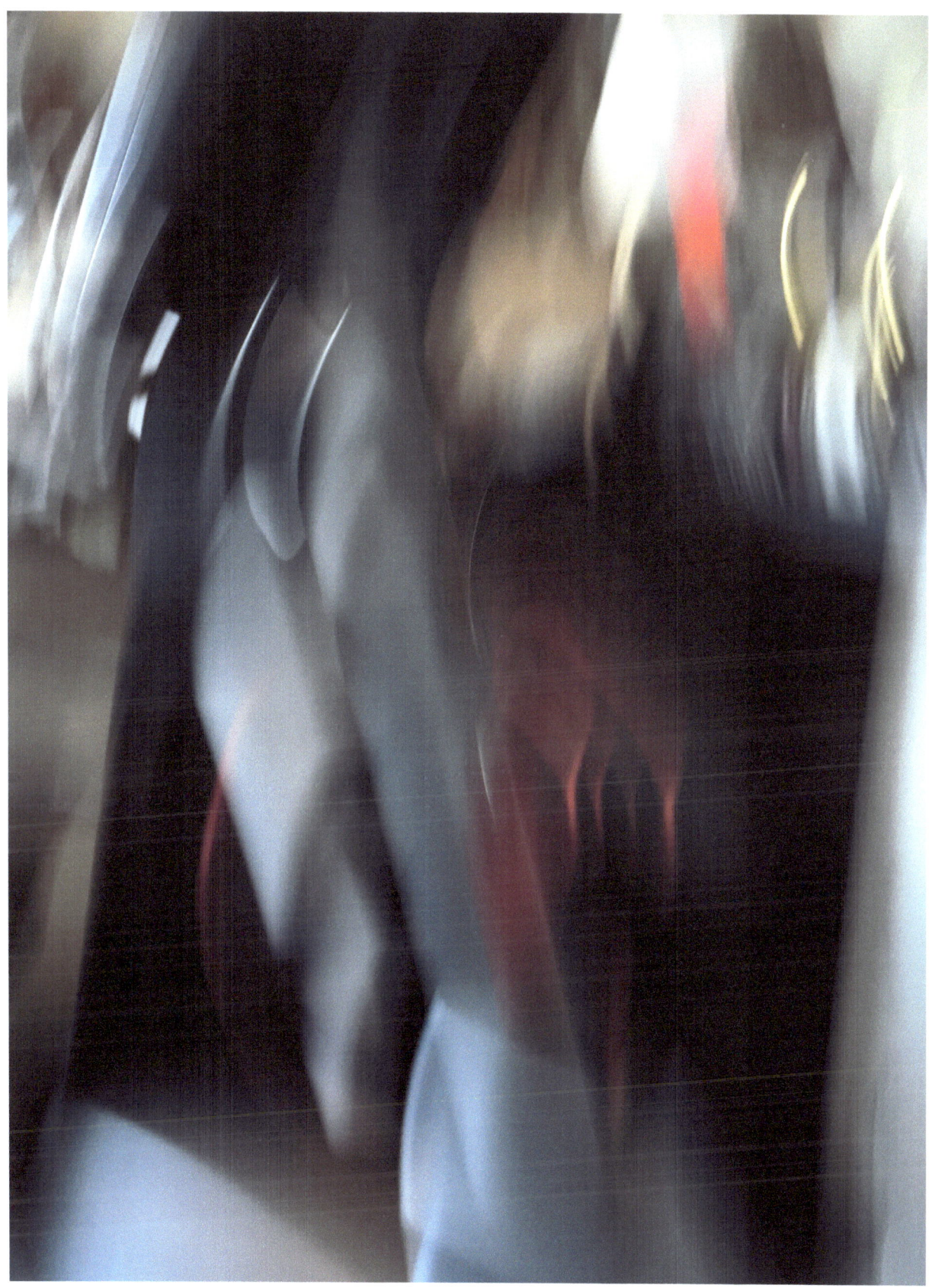

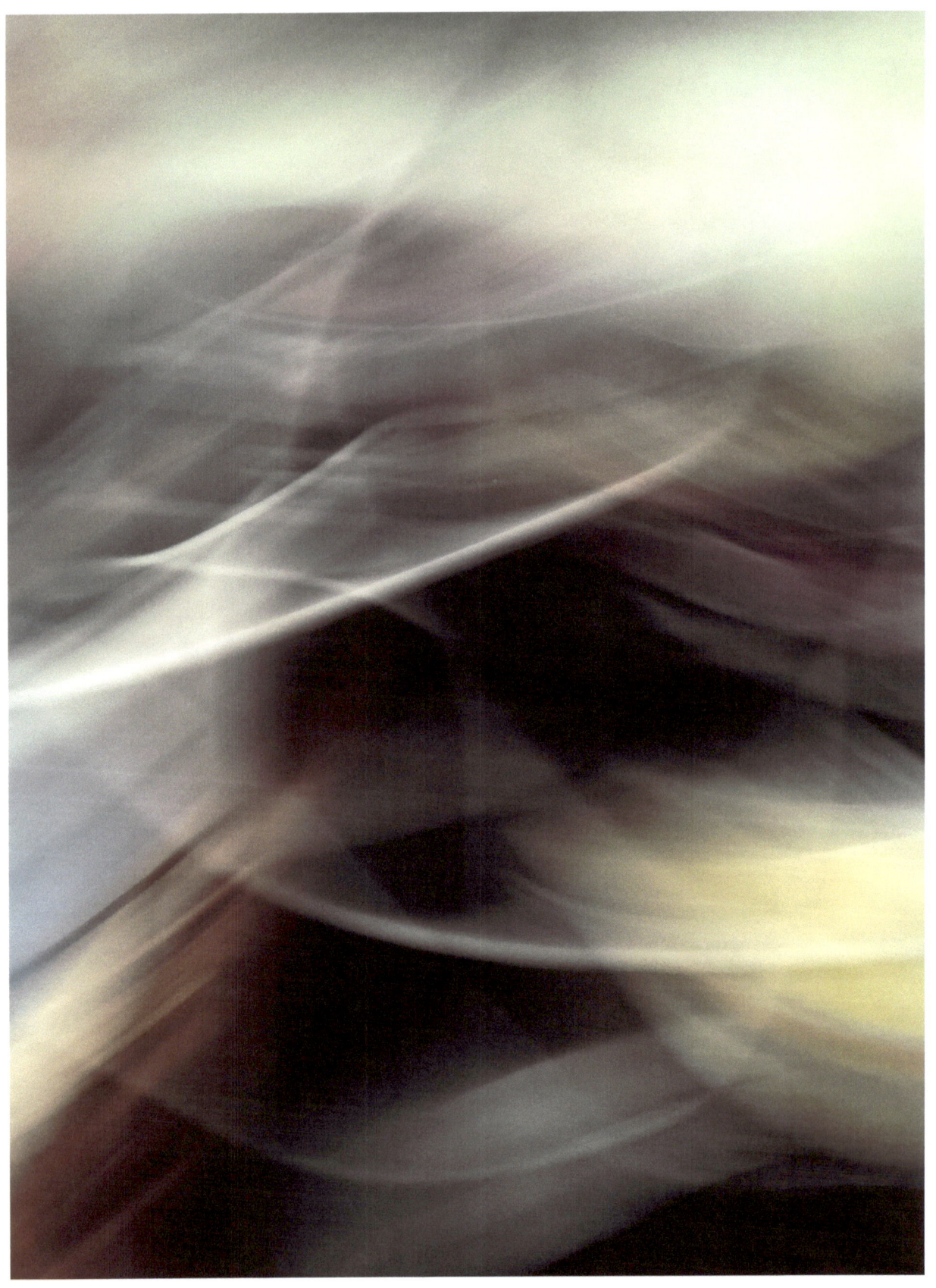

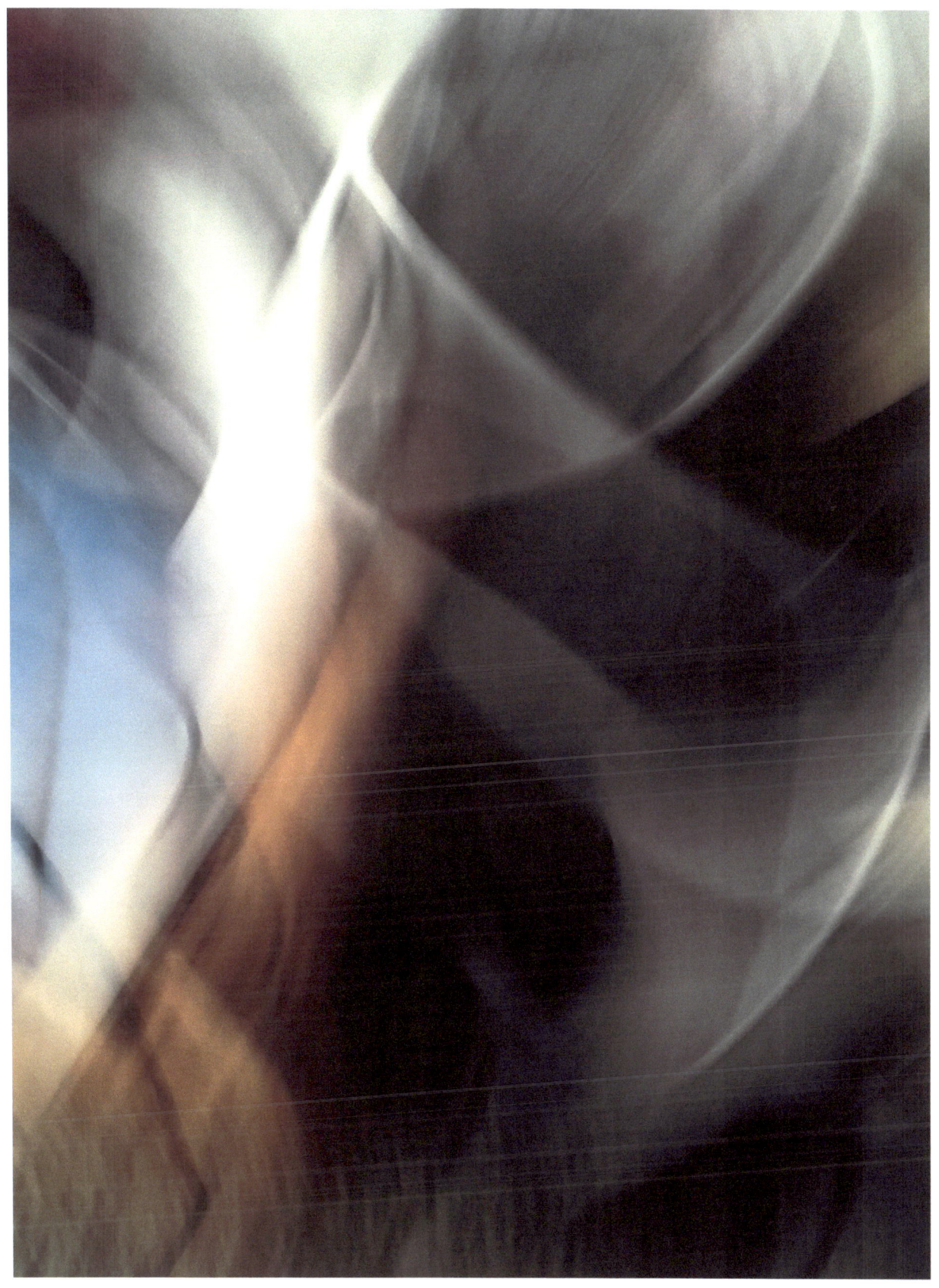

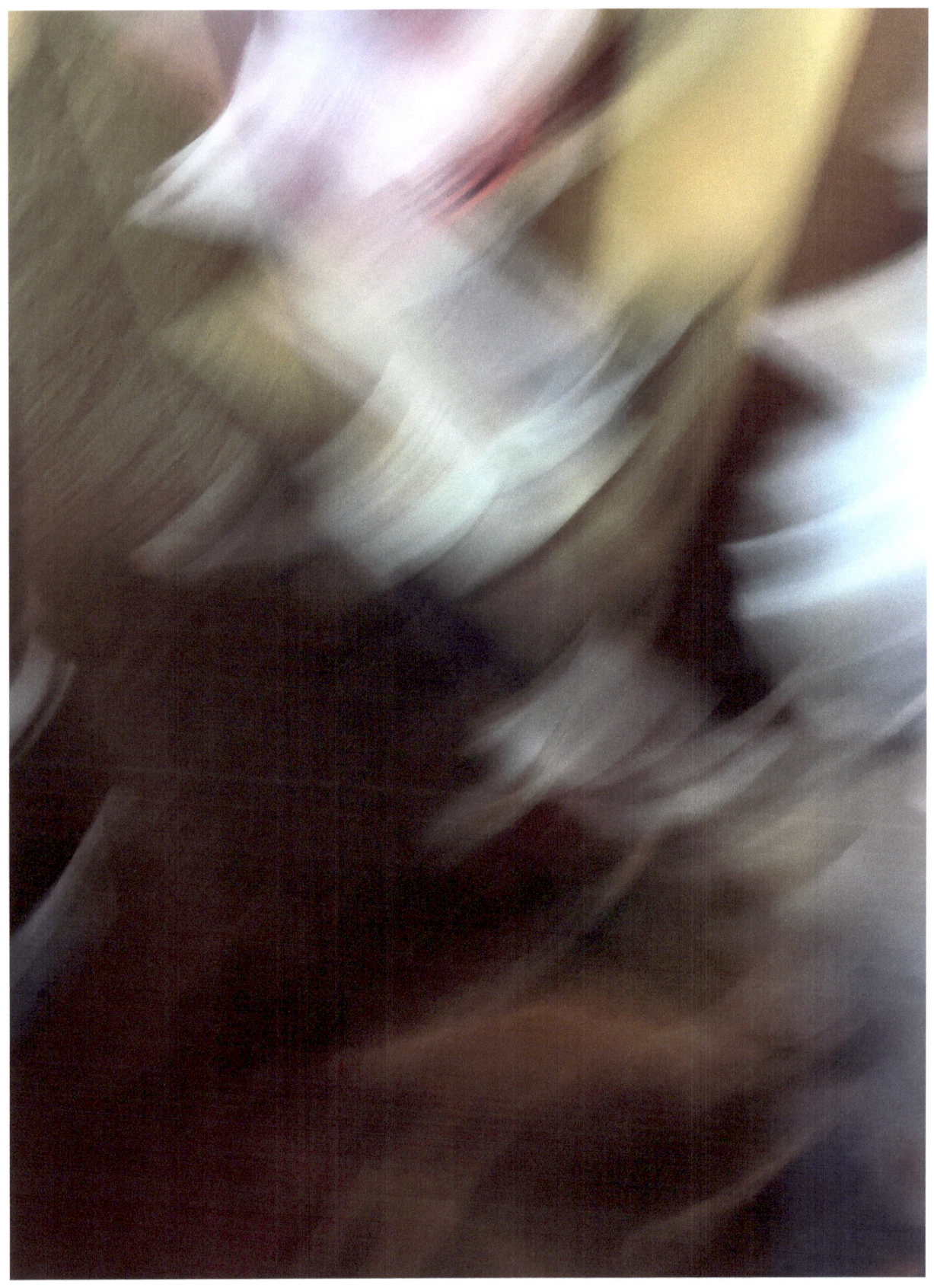

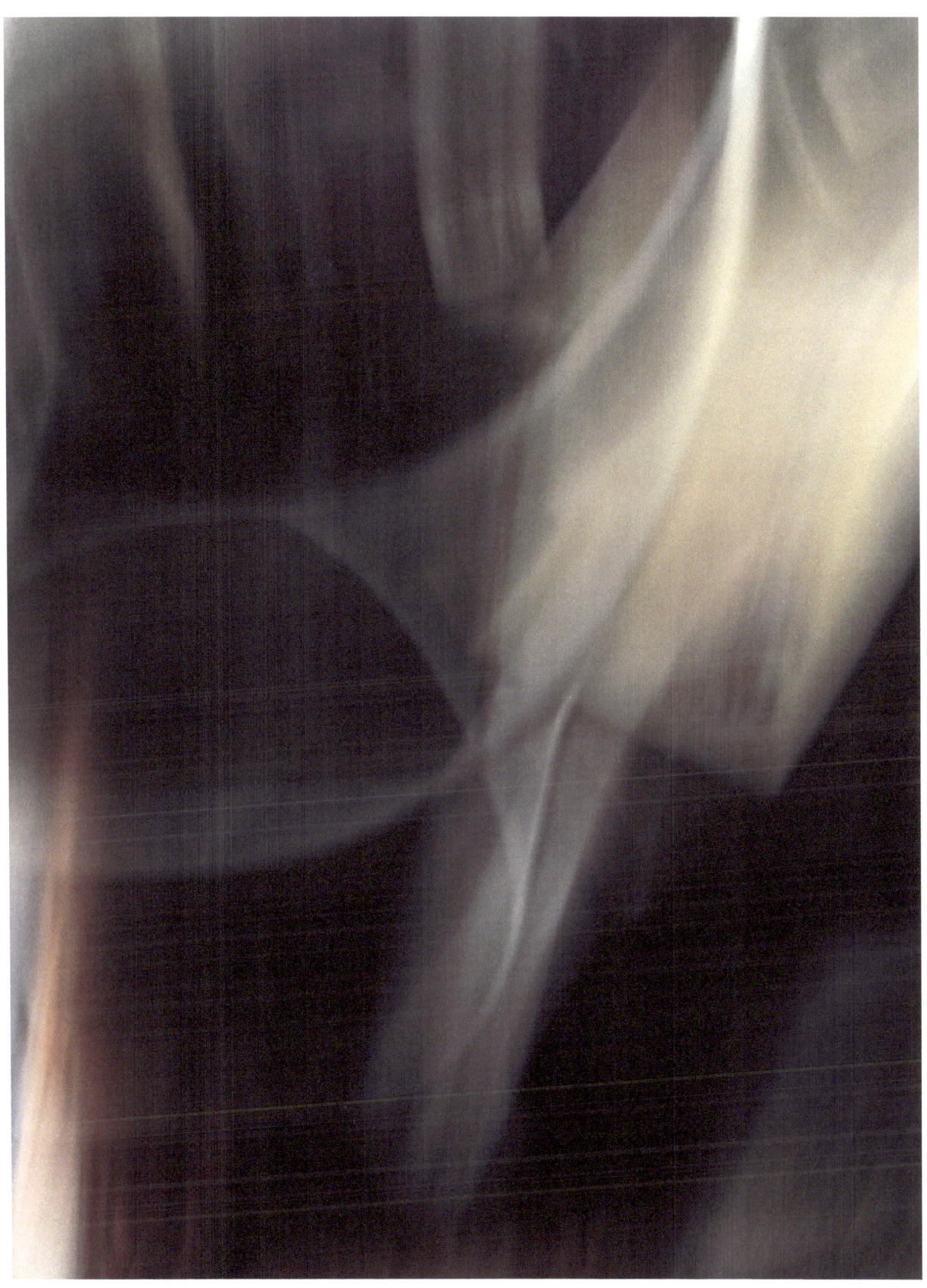

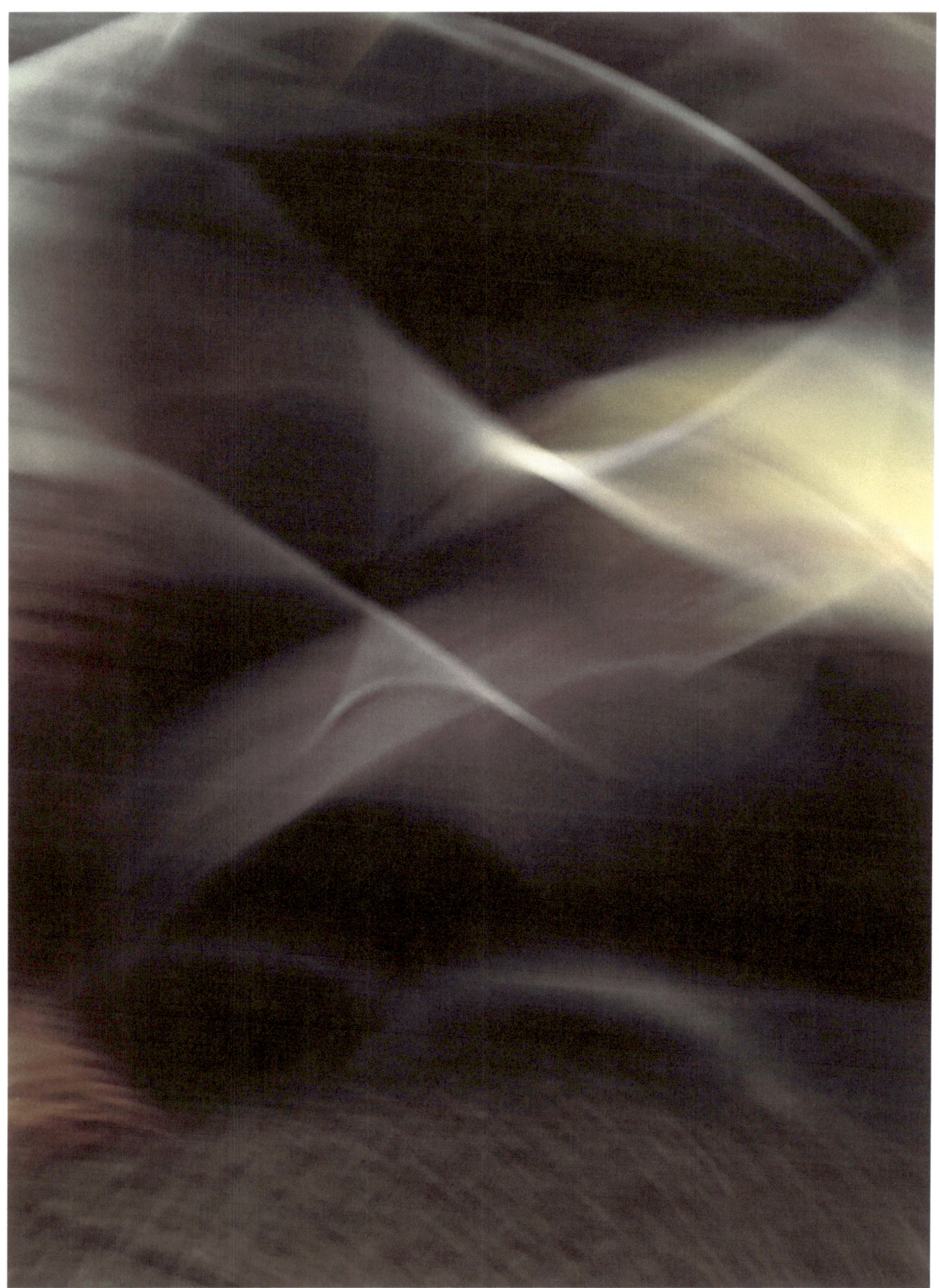

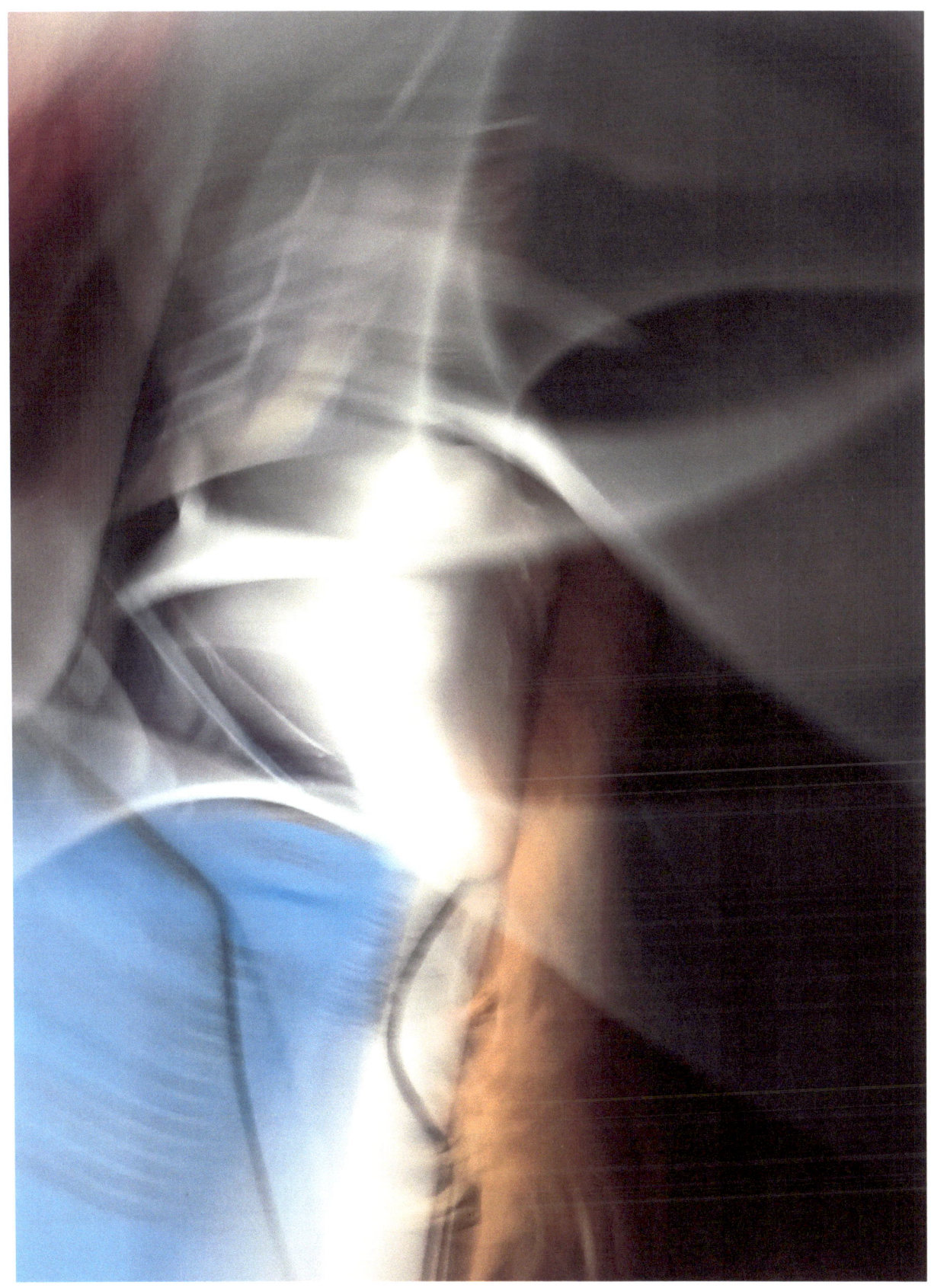

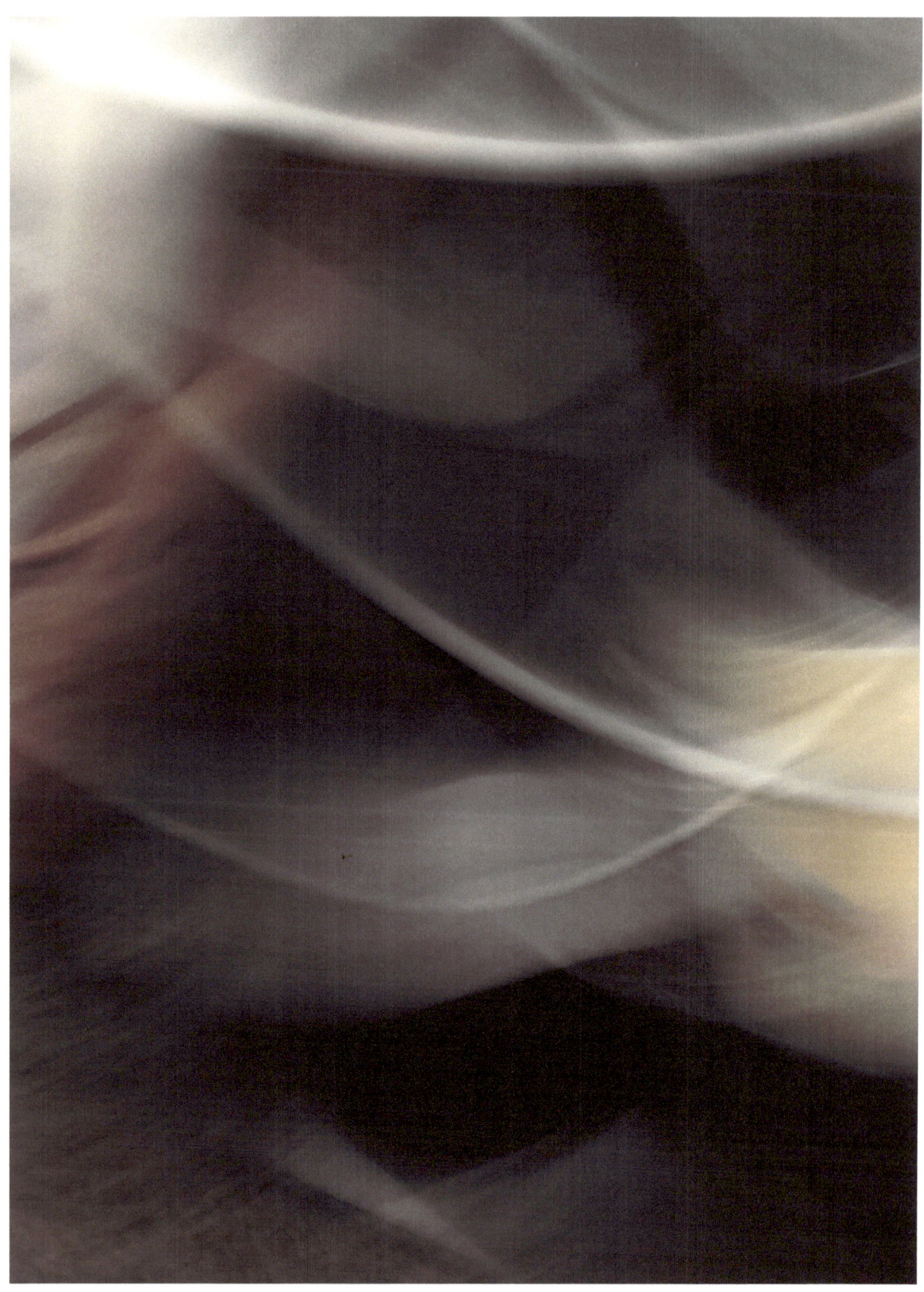

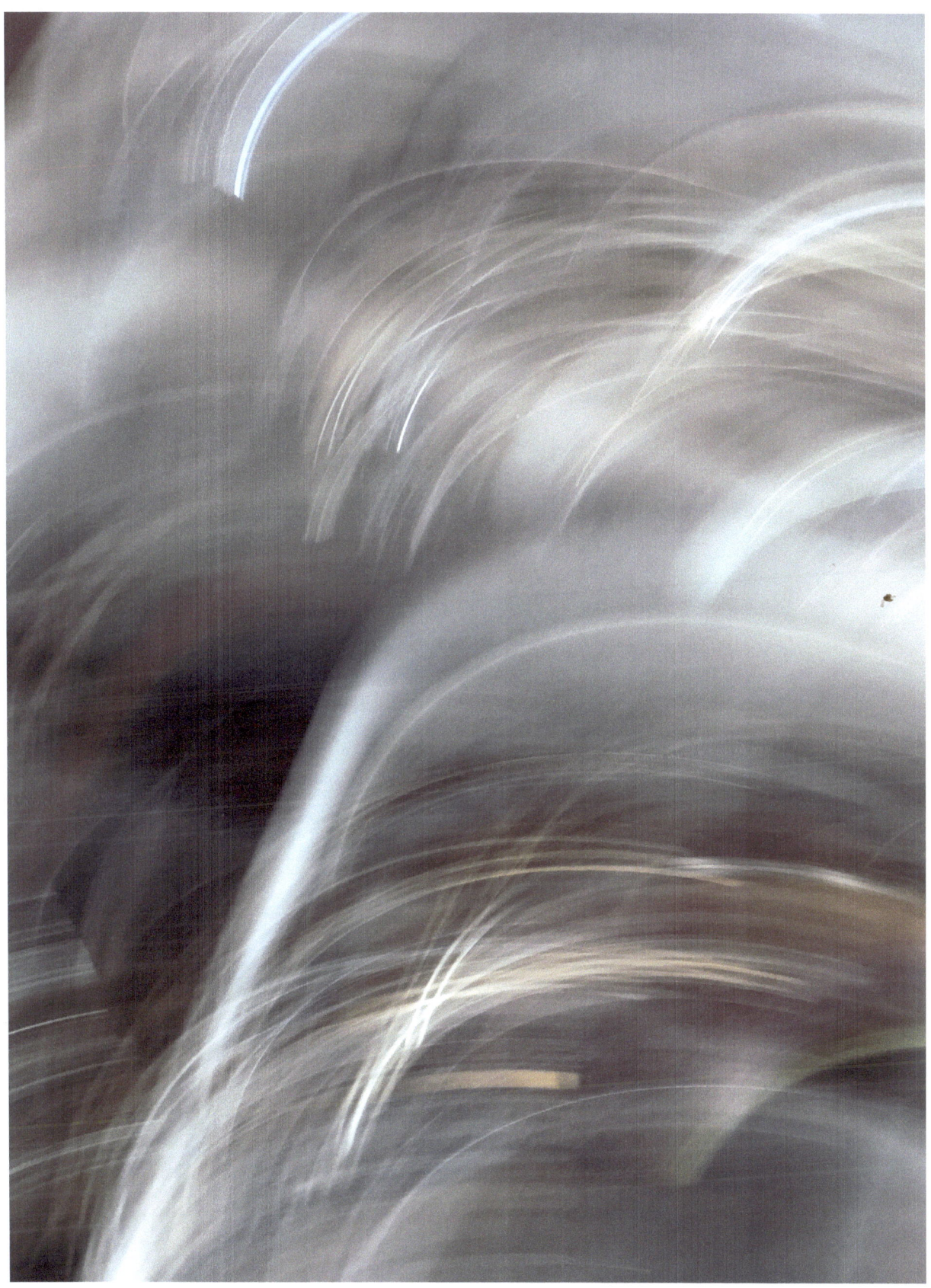

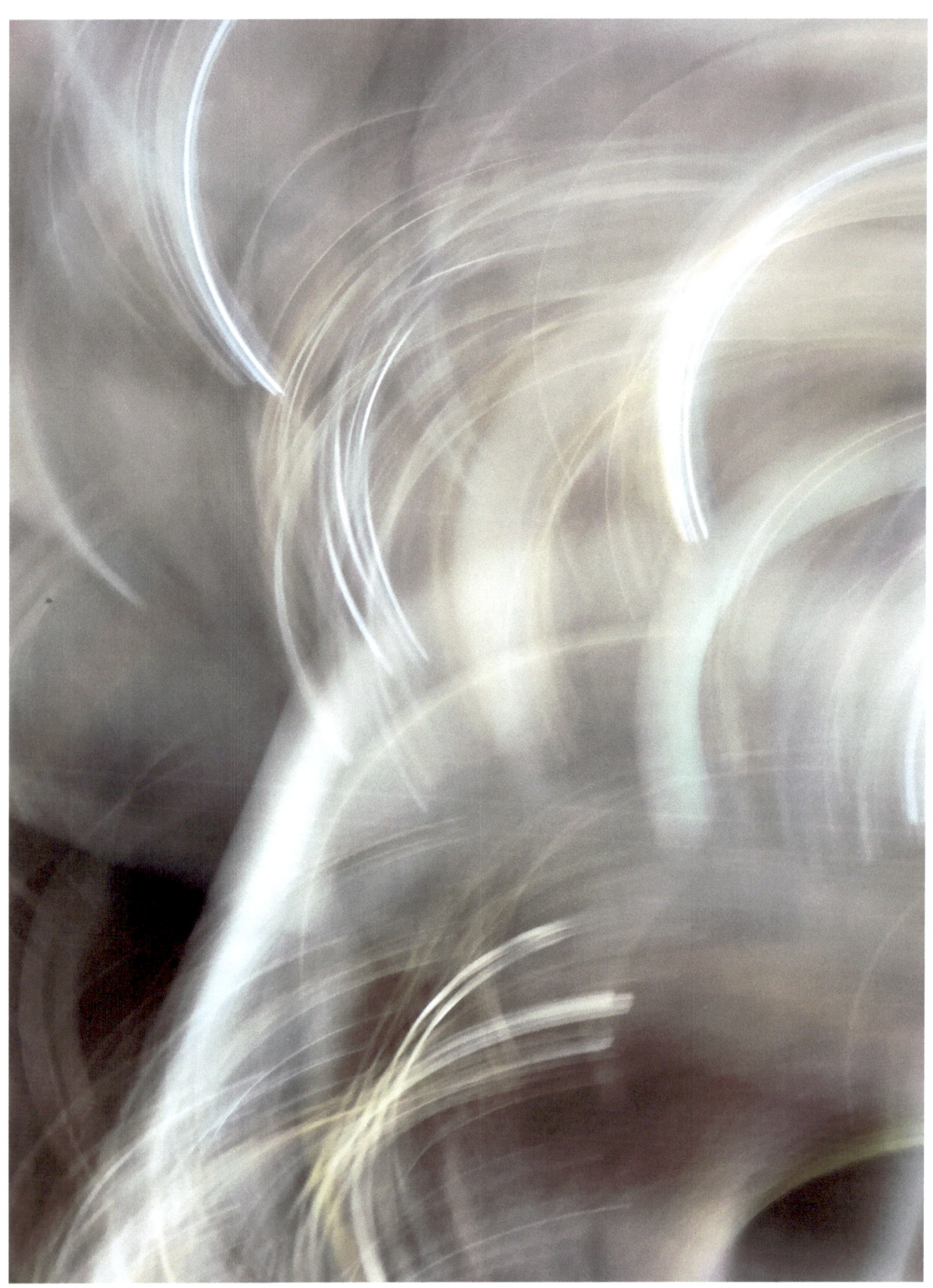

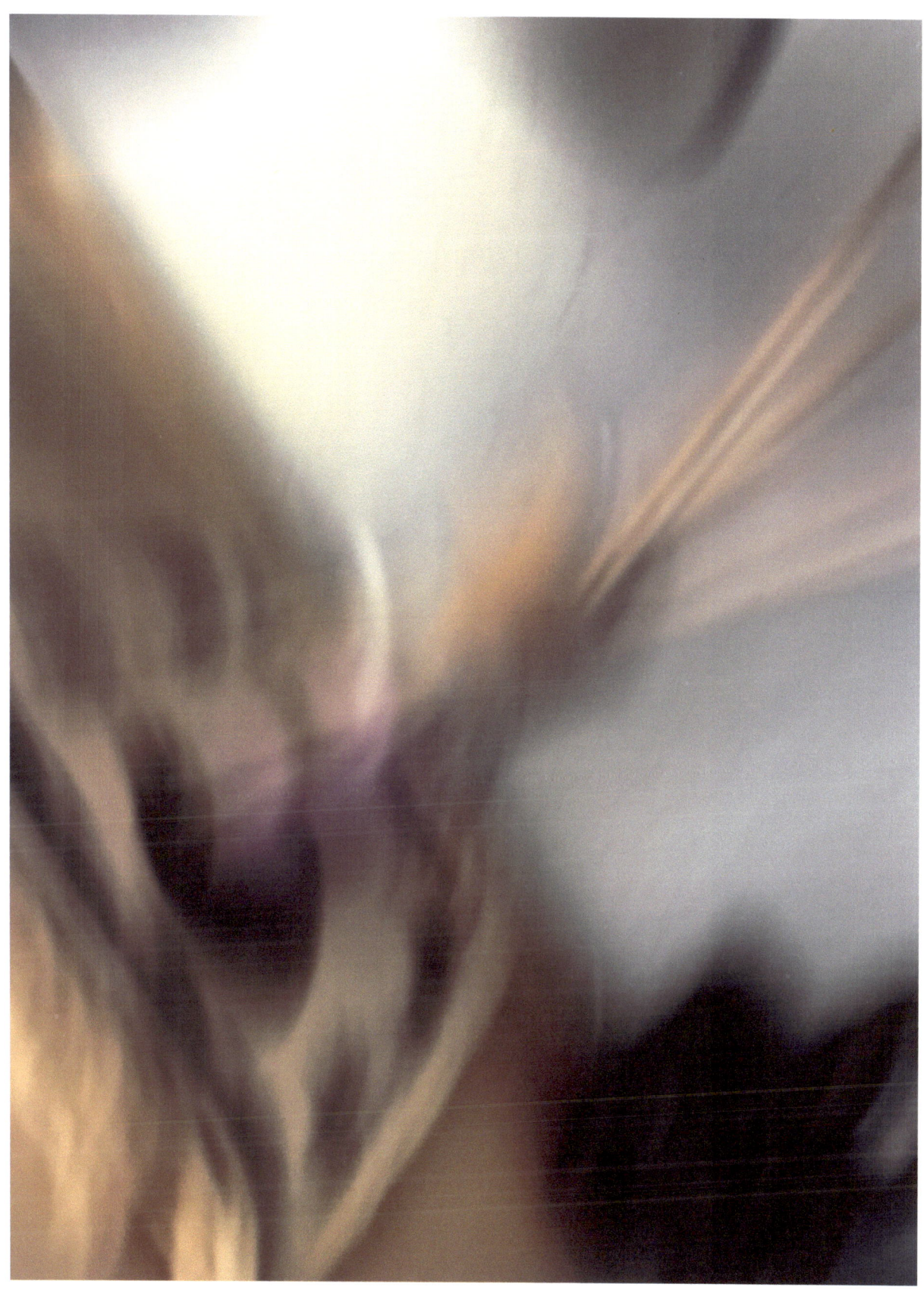

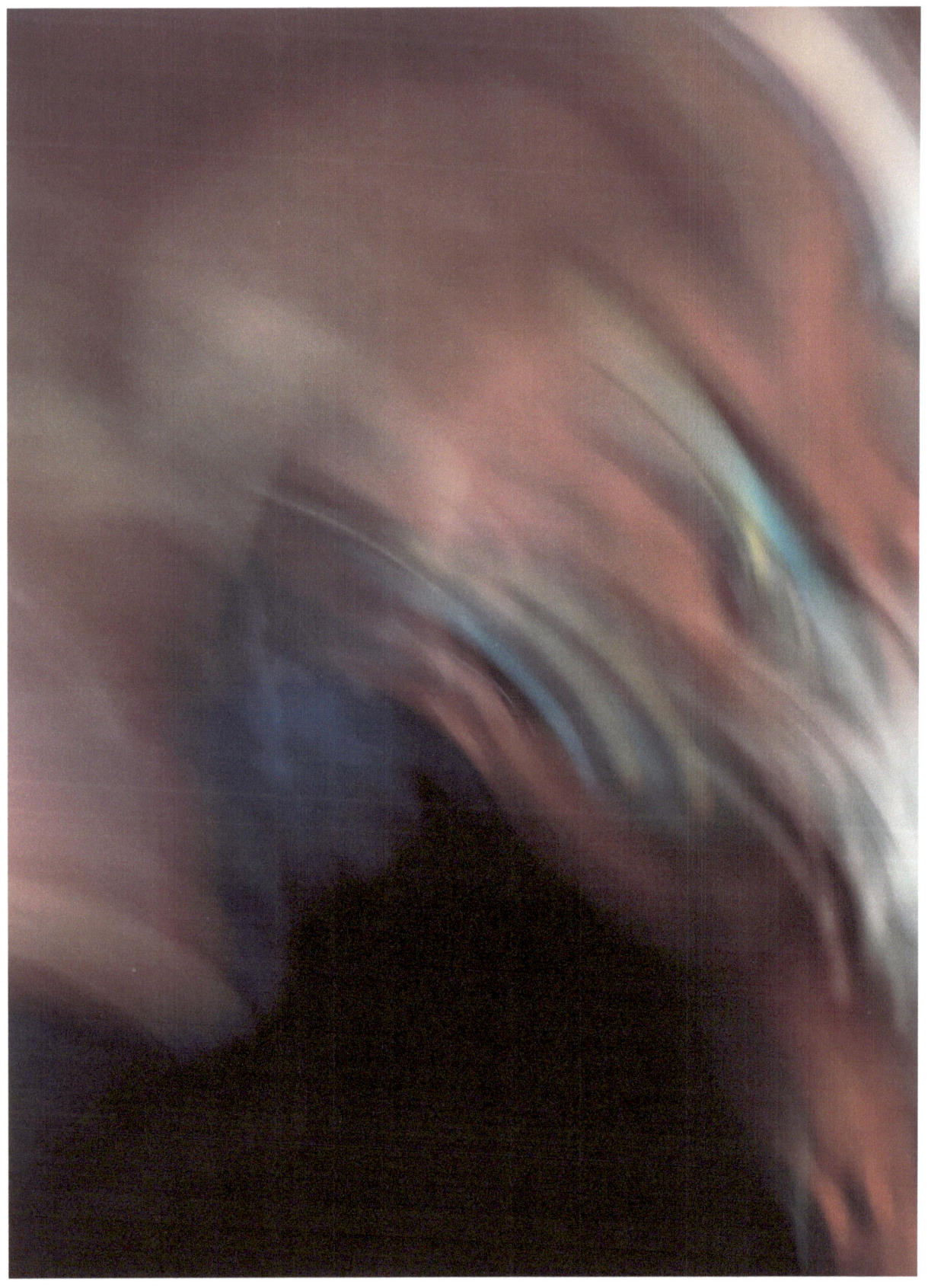

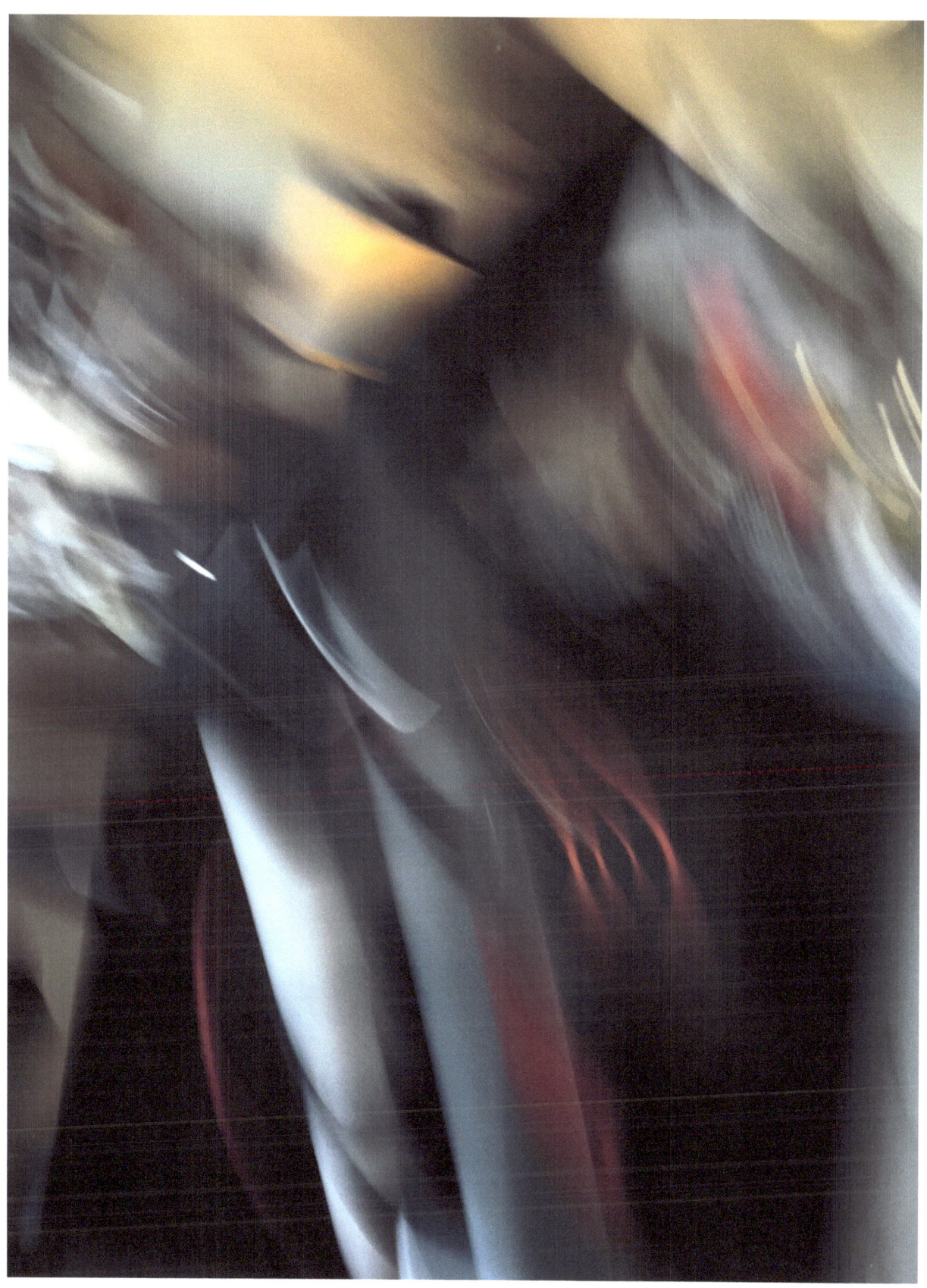

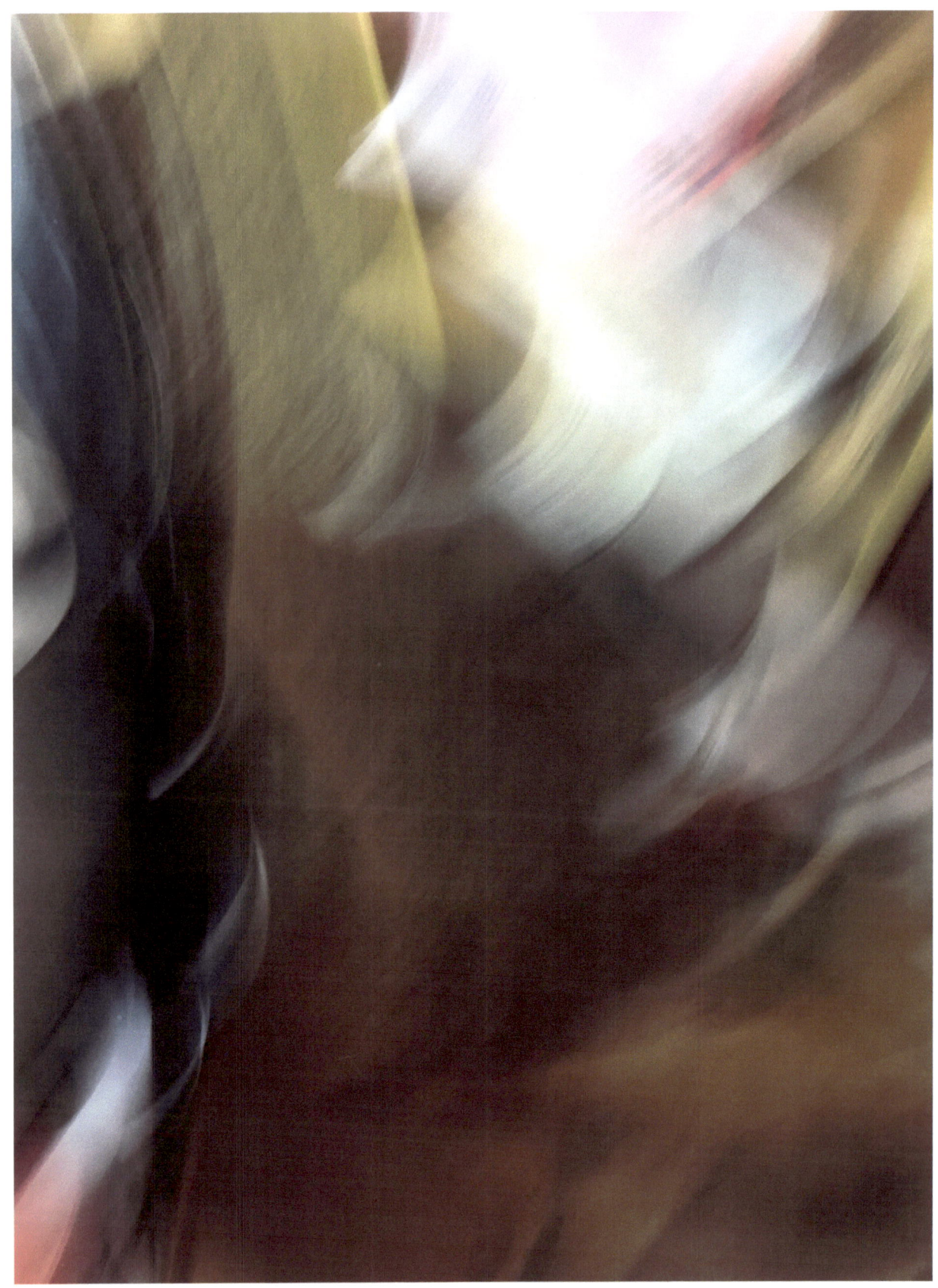

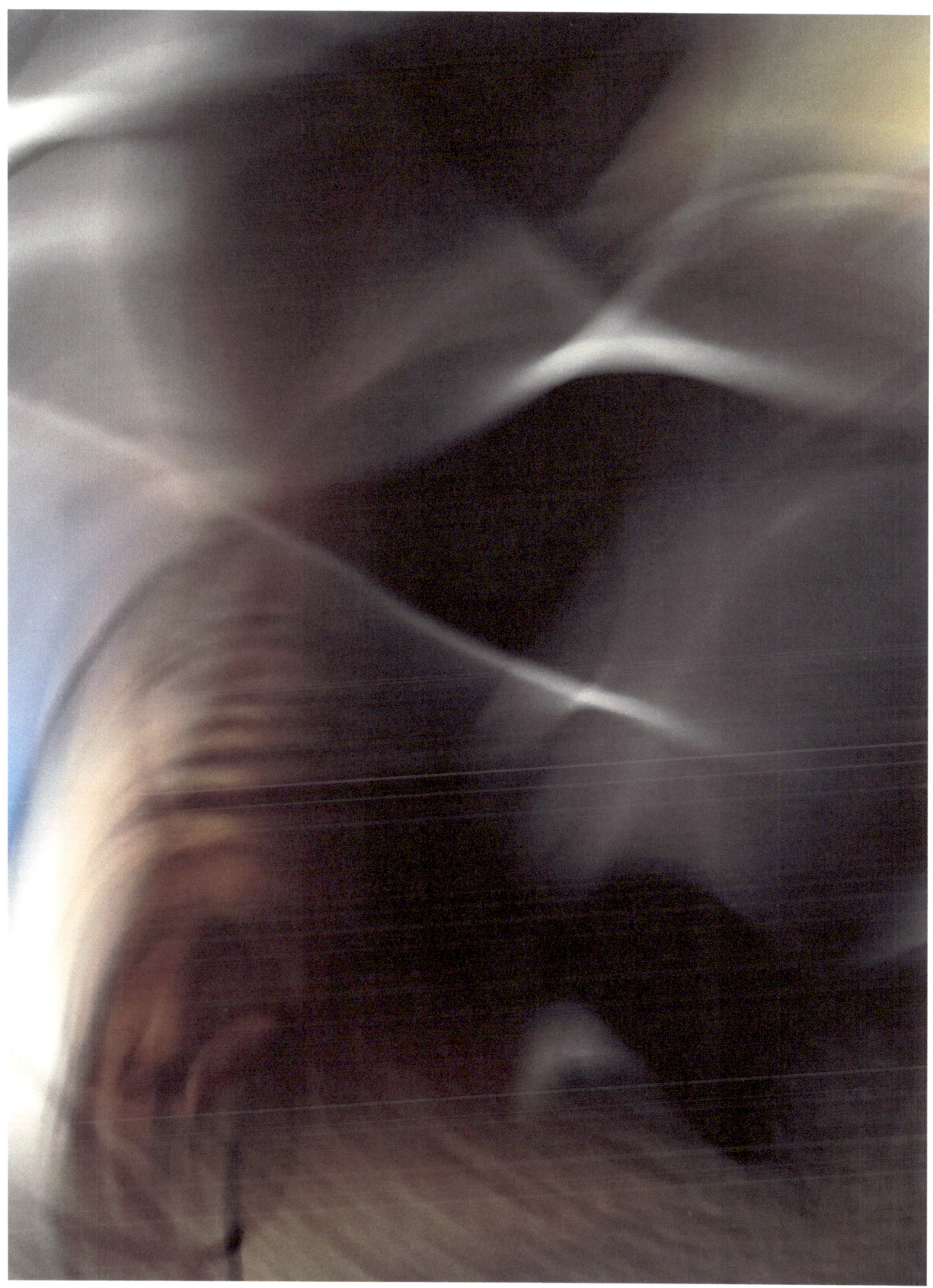

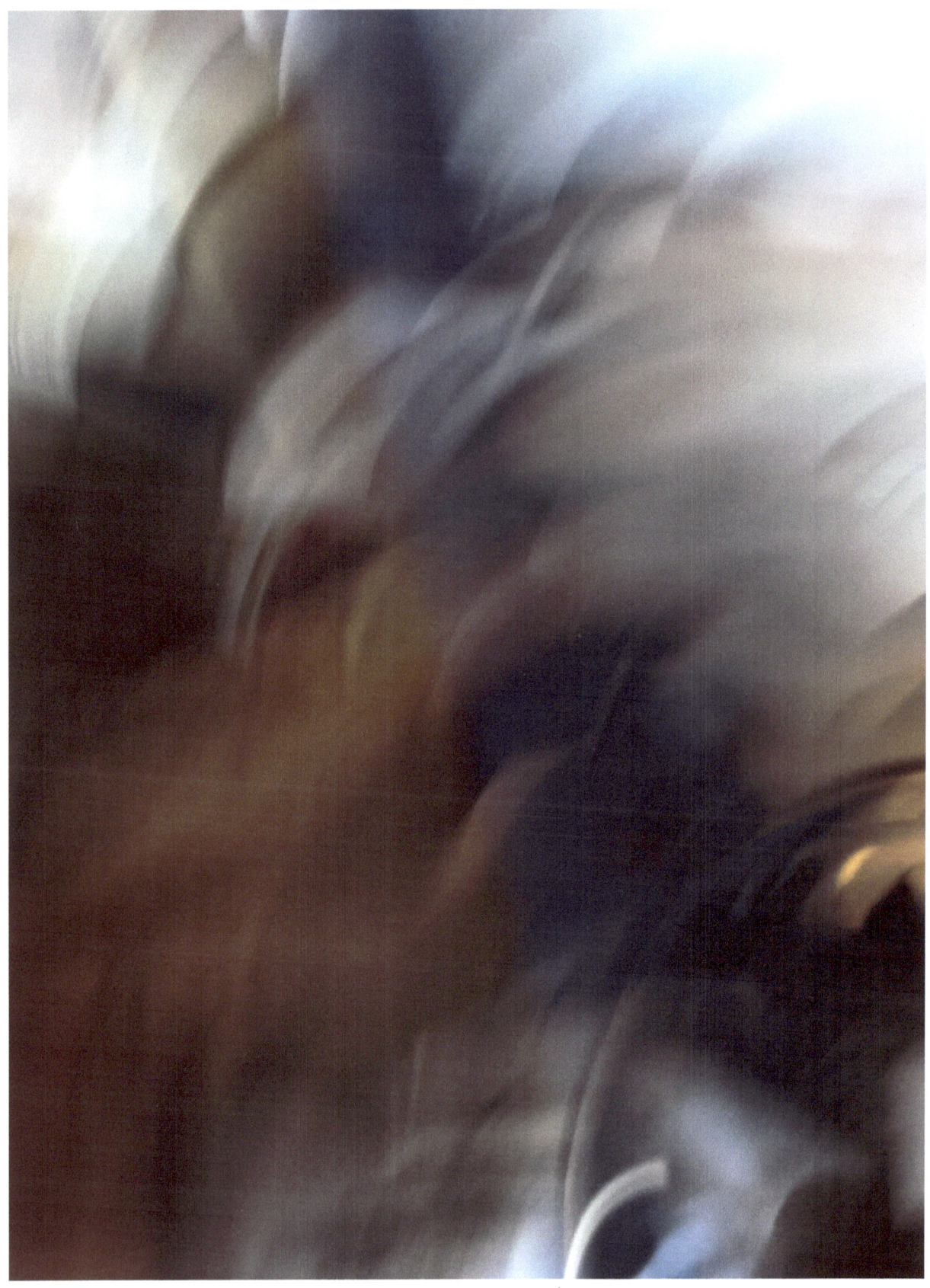

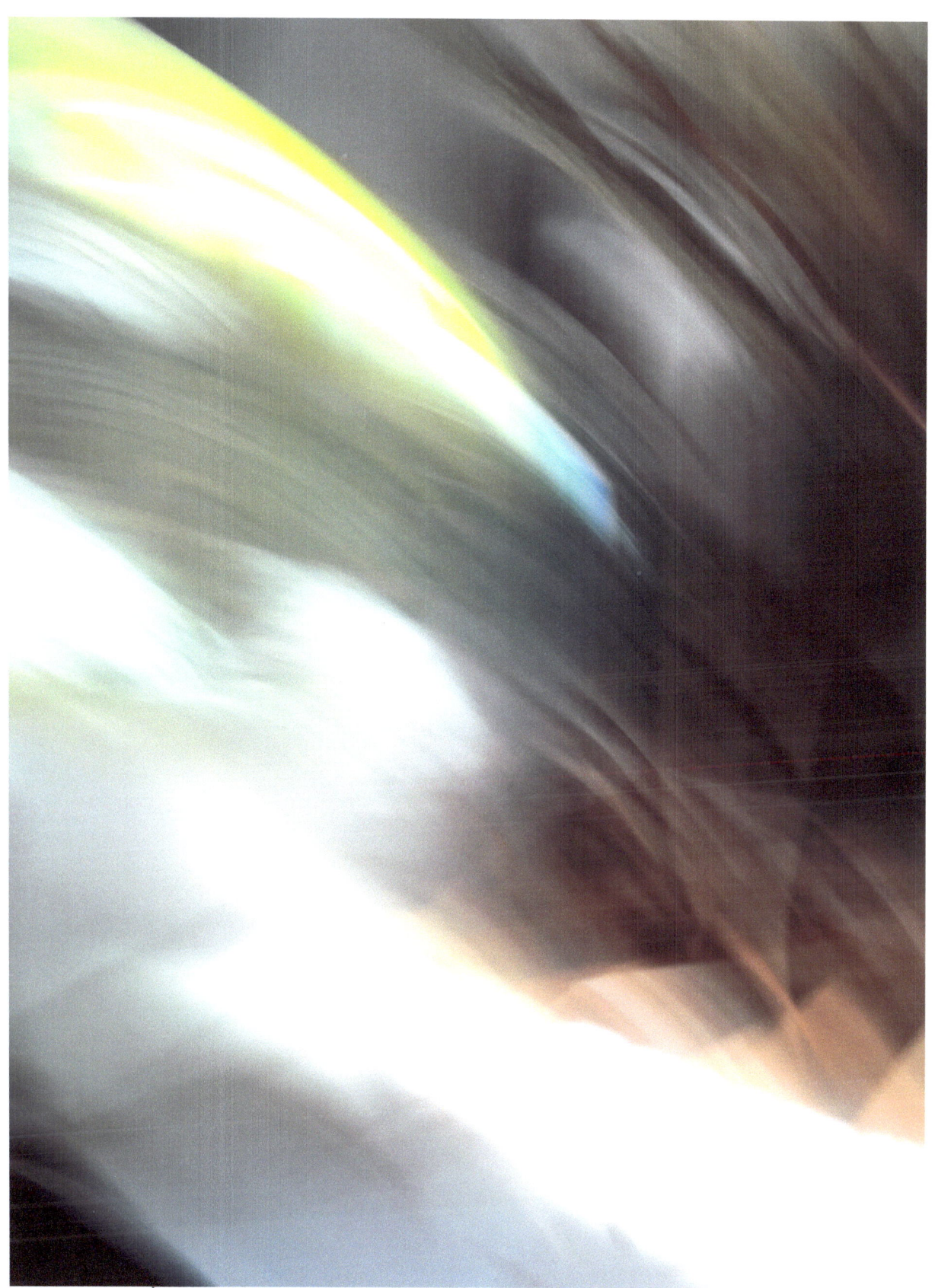

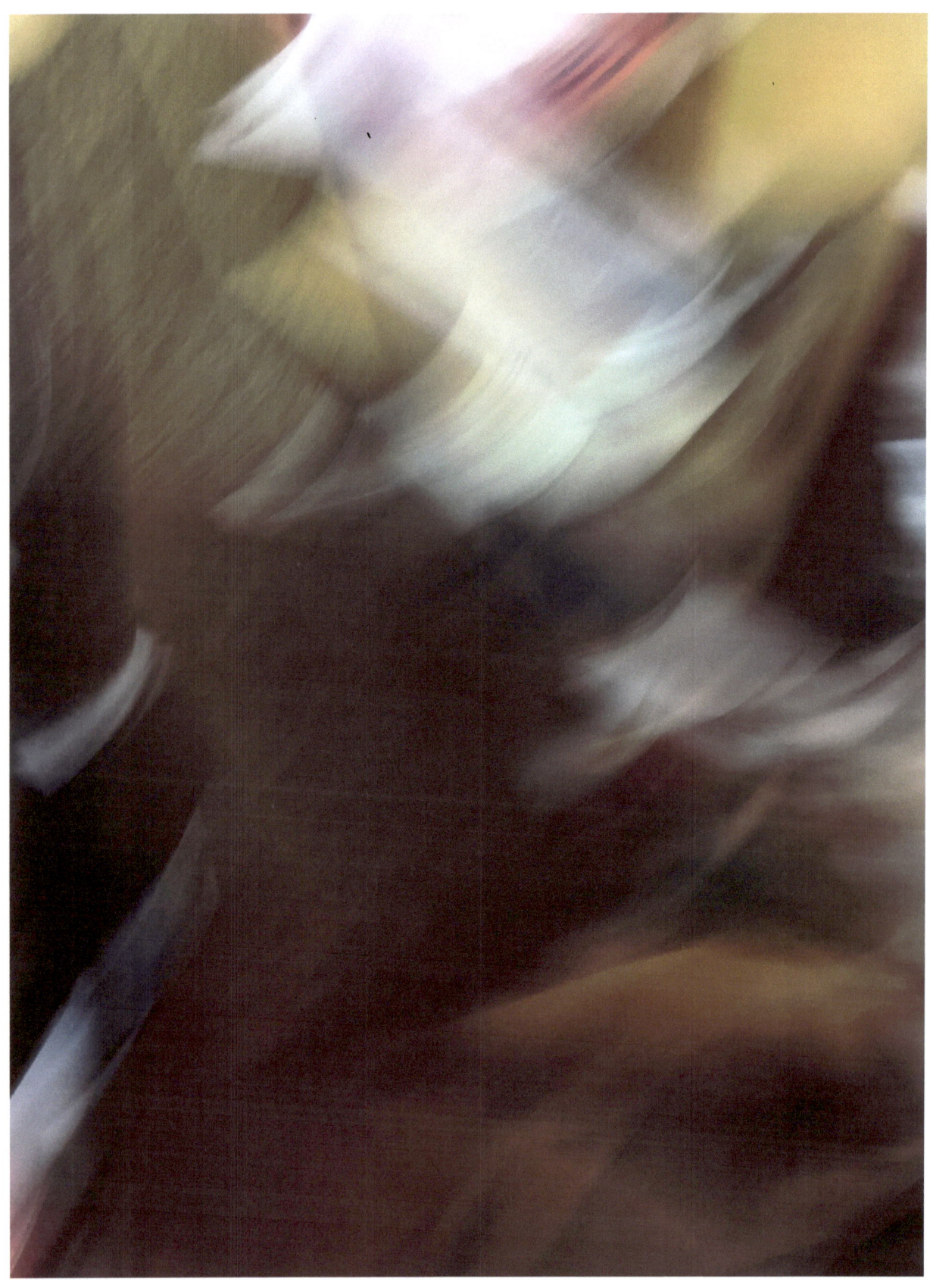

www.ingramcontent.com/pod-product-compliance
Lightning Source LLC
Chambersburg PA
CBHW050817180526
45159CB00004B/1694